INVENTING WONDERLAND

INVENTING WONDERLAND

The Lives and Fantasies of
Lewis Carroll, Edward Lear,
J. M. Barrie, Kenneth Grahame
and A. A. Milne

JACKIE WULLSCHLÄGER

THE FREE PRESS

New York   London   Toronto   Sydney   Tokyo   Singapore

THE FREE PRESS
A Division of Simon & Schuster Inc.
1230 Avenue of the Americas
New York, NY 10020

First published in Great Britain in 1995 by Methuen London,
an imprint of Reed Consumer Books Ltd.

THE FREE PRESS and colophon are trademarks
of Simon & Schuster Inc.

Manufactured in the United States of America

10 9 8 7 6 5 4 3 2 1

Library of Congress Cataloging-in-Publication data is available.

ISBN 0–684–82286–5

For William

Contents

List of Illustrations

The illustrations are reproduced by kind permission of the following:

1. The Morris L. Parish Collection of Victorian Novelists, Department of Rare Books and Special Collections, Princeton University Libraries.
2–5. The Guildford Muniment Room, Surrey Record Office.
6. The Board of Trustees of the National Museums and Galleries on Merseyside (Walker Art Gallery).
7. Islington Libraries.
10. A. & F. Pears Ltd, from an original in Unilever Historical Archives.
11, 14, 22. Bridgeman Art Library.
12. The Directors of Coutts and Co.
13. The Blackburn Museum and Art Gallery.
15, 19, 20. The Tate Gallery, London.
16. The Fine Art Society, London.
17. The Forbes Magazine Collection, New York.
18. The Royal Albert Memorial Museum, Exeter (Exeter City Museums and Art Gallery).
21. Peter Nahum at the Leicester Galleries, London.
23. The National Trust for Scotland.
24. The Beinecke Rare Book and Manuscript Library, Yale University.

25. The Royal Borough of Kensington and Chelsea.
27. The Bodleian Library.
32. The National Portrait Gallery.

The line drawings in the text are reproduced by kind permission of
the following:

pages 105 (numbers 11 and 12), 113 (number 17), 159, 164, 173,
185, 191, 199: Curtis Brown. Line drawing illustrations from *The
Wind in the Willows*, *Winnie-the-Pooh* and *The House at Pooh
Corner* by E. H. Shepard copyright under the Berne Convention.
pages 105 (number 11), 113 (number 17), 159, 164, 173: Reprinted
in Canada with the permission of Atheneum Books for Young
Readers, an imprint of Simon & Schuster Children's Publishing
Division, from *The Wind in the Willows* by Kenneth Grahame,
illustrated by Ernest H. Shepard. Copyright 1933 Charles
Scribner's Sons; copyright renewed © 1961 Ernest H. Shepard.
pages 105 (number 12), 185, 191, 199: Reprinted in Canada by
permission of Dutton Children's Books, a division of Penguin
Books USA, Inc.
pages 113, 129, 134: Illustrations by Mabel Lucie Atwell from *Peter
Pan* by permission of Hodder & Stoughton Publishers.

Acknowledgements

It is a pleasure to offer thanks to the many people who helped with the writing of this book. Among friends and colleagues, David Buckingham, Dinah Cannell, Clement Crisp, Penny Essex, Peter Higgins, Iona Opie, Alastair Macauley, Elizabeth McKellar, Deborah Steiner and Andy Stern generously shared their ideas and gave me new and valuable insights. In addition, Peter Higgins and Iona Opie made helpful and pertinent comments on the first draft of the manuscript, and greatly improved the final version.

I owe much to my editor, Pamela Edwardes, for her enthusiasm and discerning criticism, to my spirited copy-editor Tony Raven, and to my agent, Carol Heaton, who has been exceptionally supportive and sympathetic. At the Financial Times, JDF Jones, Annalena McAfee and Max Wilkinson encouraged me to develop my thoughts on children's literature in feature articles and reviews.

The staff at the British Library Manuscript Room and Reading Room and at Richmond-upon-Thames Public Library were unfailingly helpful and courteous. The curators at the Guildford Muniment Room took much trouble in showing me the collection of Lewis Carroll's papers and photographs there, and librarians at the Forbes Magazine Collection in New York kindly traced several pictures of Victorian and Edwardian children.

My mother, Maria Wullschläger, has contributed in countless ways to the writing, editing and production of the book, and I am enormously grateful to her. Her sustained interest, and the excitement and faith shown in the project by my father, Günter Wullschläger, before he died, were invaluable.

Most of all, I should like to thank my husband William Cannell for his affection, loyalty and confidence. He has always been my most perceptive and inspired critic; his ideas have shaped this book, and to him it is dedicated.

Introduction

The next best thing to being boys is to write about them.

J. M. Barrie

This book is the story of five writers who could not grow up, and who transformed their longing for childhood into a literary revolution. Lewis Carroll, Edward Lear, J. M. Barrie, Kenneth Grahame, and A. A. Milne stand at the centre of a golden age of Victorian and early twentieth-century children's books. From 1865, when *Alice's Adventures in Wonderland* became the first English children's classic, through the 1900s, when grown men cheered to hear Peter Pan declare 'I want always to be a little boy and have fun', to the nostalgic conclusion of *The House at Pooh Corner* in 1928 – 'In that enchanted place on the top of the Forest a little boy and his Bear will always be playing' – these five writers began and defined the course of our children's literature.

Their books are the great children's fantasies. *Alice's Adventures in Wonderland* and *Through the Looking-Glass*, Edward Lear's nonsense verses, *Peter Pan*, *The Wind in the Willows*, and the Winnie-the-Pooh stories are all fabulous, mythical works set in bizarre, enchanted places and peopled by peculiar creatures such as nursery-rhyme characters, playing cards, toys, talking beasts and fairies. They form a rich and distinct genre which barely existed before Lewis Carroll wrote the Alice books and has not been matched since A. A. Milne finished the Winnie-the-Pooh series. The fantastical worlds these writers created have a lasting power; Wonderland, Neverland, are physical, tangible realities from which it is hard to tear oneself away.

In these books lies a vision of childhood which still holds sway over us today. Fantasy creations have taken root among

3

the classic English social and psychological archetypes: the mad Queen of Hearts ('Off with his head'!), the honeymooning Owl and Pussy Cat, boastful, emotional Toad of Toad Hall, are all familiar characters whom we might mention in everyday conversation. 'The child who has once met Mr Badger,' wrote C. S. Lewis, 'has got ever afterwards, in its bones, a knowledge of humanity and English history.'

There are, of course, other great children's books, but none has entered the collective imagination to become popular legends in the same way as these fantasies. Their catchphrases – 'messing about in boats', 'time for a little something', 'curiouser and curiouser' – have entered common speech. Seventy years after A. A. Milne first wrote about his son's toys, we call a sulky, sad child Eeyore and a timid one Piglet. Alan Bennett's 1990 dramatisation of *The Wind in the Willows* at the Royal National Theatre was a hit among adults and children, and a comic commentary on the British obsession with class. Peter Pan, the naughty, irresponsible boy who won't grow up, lurks behind popular children's icons of the 1990s – cult singer Michael Jackson named his estate Neverland and sings 'I'm bad'; Steven Spielberg's blockbuster film *Hook* showed men behaving like boys in the boardroom.

I have chosen to explore the lives and works of the great fantasy writers as a group, in an attempt to discover the common factors which led a handful of men, between 1865 and 1930, to create a radical new literature for children of such fascination and enchantment. What made these men write this type of book at precisely that time? By comparing the lives and personalities of the five authors, and the changing social and cultural elements that moulded them, I hope to shed new light on each.

Was there a shared character trait, or fact of biography, that sparked these writers into fashioning myths of childhood? What enabled them, as adults, to see with the eyes of a child? None set out to be a children's author: Lewis Carroll was a mathematics don and Edward Lear a landscape artist; Kenneth

Grahame was a banker; J. M. Barrie and A. A. Milne were playwrights. All first told their stories casually to entertain individual children, without any thought of publication – Carroll began *Alice's Adventures* to amuse Alice Liddell, an Oxford don's daughter, on a boat trip; Grahame made up bedtime stories for his naughty son about a toad and a water rat. It is as if each writer needed a child as muse to trigger the adult imagination into creating an extraordinary fantasy. Once locked into this magical world, however, each drew on his own peculiarly strong affinity with childhood.

J. M. Barrie's self-portrait as Peter Pan speaks for all the fantasy authors. Each was a boy who did not want to grow up, who remained in part always a child. Several lost parents early and had difficult childhoods; in fantasy they tried to capture the perfect childhood they had never had. All were haunted by memories and the pastimes of youth. As adults both Lear and Grahame, for example, invented a baby language in which they corresponded with close friends. Carroll's rooms at Christ Church, Oxford, and Grahame's study in his Kensington home, were packed with toys. Milne went to Harrods' toy department specifically to search out new characters for his stories.

All shared a reluctance to engage in conventional behaviour and relationships. They were loners, in some sense social misfits, who found in fantasy an escape and an outlet to express their rage against a constricting adult society. In Lear's poem, the Owl and the Pussy Cat sail away to a paradisical land where the Bong tree grows. In the Alice books, Carroll holds up a distorted mirror to Victorian manners: a dormouse is squashed into a teapot, a pudding jumps off its plate and talks, a Queen disappears into the soup tureen. Before Carroll and Lear, children's books were educational tracts preaching conformity and obedience. Since, they have been anarchic, joky and irreverent. From Carroll's snipe at judges and the legal system ('Sentence first – verdict afterwards!') to Milne's satire on military heroism (Christopher Robin's expedition to the North Pole ends with a teddy bear sticking a pole in the ground), the fantasy writers mock adult institutions and customs.

Being childlike led all these writers to be either childless, or to have difficult relations with their children. 'He needed me to escape from being fifty', Christopher Robin Milne wrote of his father.[1] Grahame and Milne each had just one son when they were already middle-aged. Both had problems as parents, and ended life without children: Grahame's son committed suicide at the age of twenty; Christopher grew estranged from his father and saw him only twice in the years when he lay ill and dying.

Lear, Carroll and Barrie, afraid of the responsibility of becoming parents, had no children, but sought frenetically to befriend those of other people. Carroll took lone seaside holidays in order to meet little girls on the beach, sent them love letters and photographed them nude. Barrie got to know boys walking in Kensington Gardens with their nannies, played games with them and wrote a *roman-à-clef* about undressing and taking one of them to bed. Neither consciously acknowledged a sexual element in his behaviour, but today the erotic undercurrent in these friendships seems blatant.

Sexual repression is a shaping drive of the fantasies. Kenneth Grahame boasted that *The Wind in the Willows* was 'clean of the clash of sex'. *Peter Pan* celebrates the triumph of a sexless young boy over a virile grown man, Hook. In the Alice books, as William Empson observed, the idealisation of the little girl, serene and prim among voracious, sensual monsters like the Knave of Hearts and the Red Queen, depends on 'a distaste for sexuality'. Edward Lear, whose secret homosexuality set him at odds with society and whose love affair with a judge ended in disappointment and rejection, wrote fantasies about mismatched couples – the Owl and the Pussy Cat, the Duck and the Kangaroo – living happily ever after. Each child-centred fantasy offered its creator a refuge from adult problems.

Like all great artists, the fantasy writers appeared from nowhere yet could have come at no other time. For each was not only childlike, but born into a society which made a cult of childhood. The Victorian icons that gained wide popularity reveal this. All were images of eternal youth: Dickens's Little Nell, Wilde's Dorian Gray, the girl in Millais's *Cherry Ripe* and the boy in his painting *Bubbles*. The Edwardians, in a playful society headed by a playboy king, were as fixated on children's pursuits.

Since childhood was a subject at the heart of British artistic life, children's books were a natural invention of the nineteenth century. The great children's authors were men gripped personally by a longing for childhood, writing at a time when this sentiment had become a cultural phenomenon. Their obsessions took to an extreme nostalgic feelings which were shared by many of their contemporaries. In another age, their interests might have made them minor talents, but in Victorian and Edwardian England they were mainstream writers in touch with the mood of a nation, working with the unconscious force of a whole society behind them.

'It is as if', wrote the historian of childhood Philippe Aries in *Centuries of Childhood*, 'to every period of history there corresponded a privileged age and a particular division of human life: youth is the privileged age of the seventeenth century, childhood of the nineteenth, adolescence of the twentieth.' In the nineteenth century, therefore, childhood attracted major writers; the radical breakthroughs in Victorian fiction were often books which concentrated on the child – *Oliver Twist*, *Jane Eyre*, *Alice's Adventures in Wonderland*. In our century, by contrast, adolescence has been the pull: *Sons and Lovers*, *Lolita*, *The Catcher in the Rye*, with their teenage heroes and heroines, are seminal twentieth-century novels.

It is for these reasons that the rise of the children's fantasy was unique to nineteenth and early twentieth-century England, unparalleled in any other time. There is something bold and optimistic in the long summer days and golden ages of Wonderland and Neverland and the river-bank idyll of *The Wind in the Willows* which reflects the confidence and prosperity of Britain between 1860 and 1914. For all the playfulness and danger of a Queen of Hearts or a Toad or a Hook, the vision that contains them is secure, comfortable and unquestioning: Alice about to make a daisy-chain before she falls asleep dreaming of wonderland; the boy-animals Rat and Mole bathing and boating and rambling through the yellow cornfields of a sunny Edwardian afternoon; the Lost Boys walking the gangplank as Wendy announces, 'We hope our sons will die like English gentlemen', and Peter Pan crowing that 'to die will be an awfully big adventure'.

It lasted until the First World War, when to die ceased to be the awfully big adventure that Peter Pan had expected. Preoccupations changed, and after 1914 children's fantasy was not a dominant strain in British culture. A. A. Milne in the 1920s is a throwback to a pre-war idyll, nostalgically desperate to recapture the golden Edwardian era of *Peter Pan* and *The Wind in the Willows*. But after the Somme and Passchendaele, the belief was no longer there. Though Milne idealises childhood, he also mocks it. It is no accident that his characters are toys, tame household commodities rather than wild river-bank creatures or Barrie's pirates and Indians, and that their concerns are trivial jokes – the misspellings and mistakes, the fears and little deceits and vanities of six-year-olds. Milne has a palpable longing for the enchanted forest which makes his books work as myth and legend, but only just. Satire and disbelief in his own creation co-exist with nostalgia and idealism. The mix sounds the death knell of the fantasy, and makes the Pooh stories at once the last great books in the genre and the key to why they are the last.

No children's writer since Milne has created a fantasy world which has become part of everyday culture, which speaks to us of our own times and concerns. Instead, we return to these classics. 'It is only in childhood that books have any deep influence on our lives', wrote Graham Greene. The fantasies continue to enthrall: we return to them again and again, for enjoyment as children, for the consolation and humour and wisdom which their observations and jokes and stories offer adults.

1

Victorian Images
of Childhood

Whosoever shall not receive the kingdom of
God as a little child, he shall not enter therein.

The Gospel
according to St Mark, 10:15

One snowy winter's evening in the 1860s John Ruskin, soon to become Professor of Art at Oxford, received an invitation to tea from a little girl to whom he had been giving drawing lessons. Alice Liddell was the daughter of the Dean at Christ Church, and no sooner had Ruskin installed himself by the fire at the deanery than 'there was a sudden sense of some stars having been blown out by the wind', the door burst open and the Dean and his wife returned home unexpectedly early.

'How sorry you must be to see us, Mr Ruskin,' said Mrs Liddell.

'I was never more so,' Ruskin replied. The Dean suggested they continue their tea, 'and so we did,' remembered Ruskin, 'but we couldn't keep Papa and Mama out of the drawing room when they had done dinner, and I went back to Corpus, disconsolate.'[1]

It is a typical Victorian story. The respectable professional man, such as Ruskin, who idolised a pretty little girl, such as Alice, was a common figure in nineteenth-century England. Lewis Carroll, another Oxford don, became obsessed with Alice Liddell and made her famous as his child-friend and the inspiration for *Alice's Adventures in Wonderland*. Ruskin was also known for his courtship of a gifted child called Rose la Touche, nine years old when he fell in love with her. Dickens, whose child heroine Little Nell was the most loved of all Victorian fictional characters, once said that 'Little Red Riding Hood was my first love. I felt that if I could have married Little Red Riding Hood, I should have known perfect bliss.' And 'shall I confess', recorded the Victorian clergyman and diarist

Francis Kilvert, 'that I travelled ten miles today over the hills for a kiss, to kiss that child's sweet face.'[2] His rhapsody about naked young girls reflected an entire society's idea of beauty:

> One beautiful girl stood entirely naked on the sand . . . a model for a sculptor, there was the supple slender waist, the gentle dawn and tender swell of the bosom and budding breasts, the graceful rounding of the delicately beautiful limbs and above all the soft and exquisite curves of the rosy dimpled bottom and broad white thigh.[3]

The origins of English children's books lie in the Victorian romance with childhood. Men such as Carroll, Ruskin, Dickens and Kilvert took this romance to an extreme, but everywhere in nineteenth-century society and art a fascination with childhood is apparent. Reading of Little Nell's death in the serialisation of *The Old Curiosity Shop*, grown men wept openly and 'all England mourned for her'.[4] Dickens received so many bereaved letters that he felt he had committed a murder; the M.P. Daniel O'Connell, for example, reading the novel on a train, burst into tears, exclaimed, 'He should not have killed her', and threw the book out of the window. Another fictional child hero, Little Lord Fauntleroy, was so popular and influential that his velvet suit and Vandyke lace collar and curling locks became the fashionable boy's look. And Fauntleroy's contemporary, Bubbles, Millais's portrait of his little grandson blowing bubbles, became through the Pears Soap Advertisement a household name and one of the best known of all Victorian images.

This chapter sets out to trace the predominant images of childhood in nineteenth-century England, and their influence in shaping children's literature. It is the story of two new ways of looking at children which developed at this time. The first was a dawning sense of childhood as a special state, as not just a period of training for adulthood but a stage of life of value in its own right. With this, the child came to be seen as a symbol, in a prosperous, progressive society, of hope and optimism. The second was a vision of children as good, innocent and in some way connected with spirituality and imagination: an idea inherited from the Romantics, but transformed by Victorian morality, and popularised and sentimentalised. Together, these two views lay at the core of a powerful fantasy about children which adults worked out in response to their own hopes, fears and doubts about themselves and their world. It was this view of childhood which formed, and was in turn fuelled by, Victorian and Edwardian children's writers, and in particular by those who wrote fantasies.

'Enlarged sympathy with children was one of the chief contributions made by the Victorian English to real civiliza-tion', wrote G. M. Trevelyan in *English Social History*.[5] This sympathy emerged out of a growing sense in the nineteenth century of needs, desires, behaviour and rights which were distinctive to children. The Little Lord Fauntleroy costume which became so popular was part of a developing nursery culture of specific clothes, pastimes, books, toys, rules, expectations for children. 'Children's books of which the pleasure was intended to be shared with grown-ups was a characteristic invention of the time.'[5]

Portraits of children over the centuries record the evolution of a distinct nursery world in the nineteenth century. Before then, family portraits mostly show children dressed like their parents and deporting themselves with gravity and dignity as mini-adults. It was not an infant's childlike qualities, but the suggestion of his future status, that mattered. So the seventeenth-century portrait *Child with a Rattle* depicts the second Earl of Arundel as a self-confident aristocrat rather than a toddler. In a portrait of eight-year-old Charlotte Fitzroy, Charles II's illegitimate daughter, the little girl is a sophisti-cated lady in adult dress, delicately plucking a grape from a platter.

Hogarth's painting *The Graham Children* (1742), with its light tone and playful props of kitten and caged bird, demon-strates the start of a more relaxed view of children, but the sitters still wear miniature versions of their parents' dress and hold themselves with adult poise and decorum. It is only in the nineteenth century that portraits such as Millais's *Bubbles* celebrate childlike pursuits: children laugh, pout, play with toys, blow bubbles, spill milk, embrace or fight each other; their clothes and hair may be dishevelled or their behaviour unruly.

Social developments paralleled the new awareness of a specific childhood world. The 1833 Factory Act, limiting children under thirteen to eight hours work a day, was the first legal definition of childhood in terms of age in English history. Many nineteenth-century social reforms fixed on children, and charities – the Shaftesbury Society, the Society for the Prevention of Cruelty to Children – were founded to protect their interests. Education became more widely available, and by 1870 an Education Act was passed which for the first time envisaged education becoming universal and compulsory. Partly as a result, there developed a perception of children as agents of social mobility in a way which would have been impossible in pre-industrial England. In an environment of commercial and industrial expansion and progress, the child was a focus for the aspirations of a prosperous, forward-looking society.

This was especially true of the economically powerful middle classes who drove Victorian England. Humanist families like the Arnolds and the Huxleys and the Stephens, who believed in learning and self-improvement, governed British intellectual life. Queen Victoria favoured middle-class pursuits; in contrast to her decadent, philandering and extravagant Hanoverian predecessors, she set an example of cosy family gatherings and the enjoyment of homely pleasures like card games and Christmas trees. From the top of society through the urban middle class, family life was seen as an ideal.

Ruskin called the home 'a sacred place, a vestal temple, a temple of the hearth watched over by Household Gods'. William Frith's painting *Many Happy Returns of the Day*, with its birthday girl sitting in a halo of flowers amid playing children and admiring adults, is a celebration of middle-class family ritual. William Mulready's famous picture *The Lesson*, where a child sits on his mother's lap in the pose of a Renaissance Madonna and Child, is an adoration of contemporary motherhood. As its devotional connotation suggests, idealising the family was in part a substitute for religious faith. It was widely feared in the nineteenth century that the decline in religious belief would lead to amorality and social anarchy, and many people sought an alternative, secular moral code to guard against chaos and unbridled licence. Family values implied social and sexual stability, children suggested innocence and purity; both were important in the new humanist morality.

At the same time, as families grew smaller, parent–child relationships became closer and adults focused more intensely on children. What we call the nuclear family, with its generally higher level of complex relationships and neurosis, began in the nineteenth century. Middle-class mothers, no longer ceaselessly pregnant or nursing, were able to spend time on their children as individuals, and chose to do so. The bestselling Victorian novelist Mrs Humphry Ward, who in the 1870s had three well-spaced children – as opposed to her mother's nine and her mother-in-law's seventeen – rejoiced that her generation 'wheeled their own perambulators in the Parks . . . bathed and dressed and taught their children'.[6] The lives of the children's authors are typical here. Edward Lear, born in 1812, was one of twenty-one children and barely knew his mother, who left him to be brought up by sisters. A. A. Milne, a late Victorian born in 1882, was one of three children brought up in a close-knit family by supportive parents who encouraged academic ambition and devoted their lives to their boys.

Around this type of family a new commerce grew up. 'The sympathetic interest in the games, fancies and thoughts of children', Trevelyan wrote, 'was one of the best features of an age that thought much of family life.'[7] Mass production and middle-class prosperity together created a huge increase in children's toys, clothes and books. A painting of the Lowther Arcade, a covered walkway of toy shops in central London on a site now occupied by Coutts Bank, shows the Victorian family out to play: children blowing trumpets and beating drums, eager mothers investigating dolls with their daughters, benign fathers sweeping down a gallery awash with rocking horses and tambourines and magic lanterns. Children's books, one of the most profitable parts of the Victorian publishing industry, belonged to this world, and were imbedded in middle-class culture.

Lewis Carroll, hoping for a wide middle-class readership for *Alice*, advised his publishers that 'below that I don't think it would be appreciated'.[8] When his well-bred heroine falls down a rabbit hole, one of her fears is that she is transformed into a lower-class girl: 'I must be Mabel after all, and I shall have to go and live in that poky little house, and have next to no toys to play with.' The upper-middle-class superiority of characters from Alice to the Darling children in their frilly Bloomsbury nursery, from Badger and Water Rat fighting off the proletarian stoats and weasels in *The Wind in the Willows* to Beatrix Potter's elegant gentlemen frog and newt Mr Jeremy Fisher and Sir Isaac Newton, suggests how at ease Victorian and Edwardian children's writers were with contemporary social structures. The national self-confidence, the assumption that the status quo would continue, the belief in the future which made the child a natural icon, all are in the background. It was the perfect climate for a golden age of children's books.

Between 1837, when Queen Victoria came to the throne, and the beginning of the First World War in 1914, almost all the books we now regard as children's classics were published: *Alice's Adventures in Wonderland* and *Through the Looking-Glass*; Edward Lear's nonsense poems, E. E. Nesbit's Bastable stories and *The Railway Children*, Frances Hodgson Burnett's *Little Lord Fauntleroy* and *The Secret Garden*, Stevenson's *Treasure Island*, Kenneth Grahame's *The Wind in the Willows*, J. M. Barrie's *Peter Pan*, Beatrix Potter's Peter Rabbit tales, Kipling's *Stalkey & Co* and the *Just So Stories*. Although classic stories for children also appeared in Europe and America around this time – Hoffmann's *Nutcracker and*

Mouse King, the inspiration for Tchaikovsky's ballet; Hans Christian Andersen's tales; Louisa Alcott's *Little Women*; Joanna Spyri's *Heidi* – no other country experienced a golden age of children's literature comparable to that in England.

The settings of the Victorian and Edwardian children's classics themselves suggest the mood of a golden age, of a secure, prosperous, optimistic country. Yet Wonderland, the Neverland of Peter Pan, the river bank of *The Wind in the Willows*, the idyll of a country station in *The Railway Children*, the enchanted rose garden in *The Secret Garden*, all also celebrate escape, the flight into an unreal dream world. They point to one of the strongest influences on the Victorian and Edwardian cult of childhood and on children's books: the regressive desire for a pre-industrial, rural world and the identification of the child with purity, a pre-sexual life, moral simplicity.

The symbolic association between childhood, innocence and regeneration is age-old, lying at the heart of the New Testament and of Christian thought; Christians worship their god as a new-born baby, children are emblems of purity and faith in Shakespeare and Dante, and important images for mystical writers such as Thomas Traherne. But the nineteenth century, taking on the Romantic interpretation of Blake and Wordsworth and the focus on nature, transformed the image by relating it specifically to contemporary society and morality. For the first time, these ideas about childhood penetrated secular culture on a mass scale.

The Romantic view of childhood as a privileged and seminal state, connected with both spiritual redemption and the natural world, was inherited from the French philosopher Rousseau's concept of man as a 'noble savage', and set out by Wordsworth in his ode to youth, 'Intimations of Immortality':

> And not in utter nakedness,
> But trailing clouds of glory do we come
>   From God, who is our home:
> Heaven lies about us in our infancy!
> Shades of the prison-house begin to close
>   Upon the growing Boy,

> But he beholds the light, and whence it flows,
>> He sees it in his joy;
> The Youth, who daily farther from the east
>> Must travel, still is Nature's priest,
>>> And by the vision splendid
>>> Is on his way attended;
> At length the Man perceives it die away,
> And fade into the light of common day.

Before the Romantics, children did not feature significantly in English literature. With Blake and Wordsworth, they became for the first time central characters – in Blake's poems such as 'Infant Sorrow' and 'The Little Black Boy', where the speakers are children; in Wordsworth's Lucy poems, which celebrate the life of an unknown three-year-old country girl. Adopting the Romantic creed that 'the Child is father of the Man', Victorian writers continued this focus on children and brought it to a peak. Oliver Twist, the first child-hero in the English novel, appeared in 1837, the year Victoria became Queen. Child characters – David Copperfield, Jane Eyre, Heathcliff and Cathy, Tom and Maggie Tulliver – soon dominated Victorian fiction.

Children's books were the natural next step. Literary fairy tales such as Ruskin's *The King of the Golden River* began to be written in the 1840s and 50s; fantasy stories for children became widely popular in the 1860s and 70s with *Alice's Adventures in Wonderland* and *Through the Looking-Glass*, Charles Kingsley's *The Water Babies*, George MacDonald's *Dealing with Fairies* and *At the Back of the North Wind*, and Christina Rossetti's *Speaking Likenesses*. All starred child heroes or heroines and many depended on the Romantic idea that the child has an imaginative vision superior to that of adults, and so can perceive fantasy characters or landscapes to which adults have no access. It was a theme which was still strong in Edwardian writing – in *Peter Pan*, children are free because they can fly and thus reach Neverland, while adults remain rooted in the Kensington nursery. Barrie's nostalgic lines in *Peter Pan and Wendy* (1911):

On these magic shores children at play are forever beaching their coracles. We too have been there; we can still hear the sound of the surf, though we shall land no more.

echo Wordsworth's vision in his 'Intimations of Immortality':

> Hence in a season of calm weather
>   Though inland far we be,
> Our souls have sight of that immortal sea
>   Which brought us hither,
>   Can in a moment travel thither,
> And see the children sport upon the shore,
> And hear the mighty waters rolling evermore.

Much in nineteenth and early twentieth-century art suggests the central and adored place of children in the Victorian and Edwardian psyche. In Lawrence Alma-Tadema's *Earthly Paradise*, a woman kneels and kisses the hand of a cherubic naked baby; in William Orchardson's *Her Idol*, a mother sits transfixed by her little daughter, who in turn is absorbed in her doll. Browning's poem 'The Pied Piper of Hamlyn' celebrates the seduction of a whole townful of boys and girls. The subjects painted by Millais, most popular of all Victorian artists, included *My First Sermon* and *My Second Sermon*, *Little Red Riding Hood*, *The Boyhood of Raleigh*, *Cinderella*, *The Orphans*, *Bubbles*, and *Cherry Ripe*. When *Cherry Ripe*, a picture of a little milkmaid with a handkerchief of cherries in her lap, was published in *The Graphic* for Christmas 1879, the print run of 600,000 sold out overnight.

Cherry Ripe illustrates how Victorian artists maintained the Romantic link between childhood, nature and natural goodness, but overlaid it with mawkishness and morality: the little country girl is an image of sexual purity. A favourite theme at the time was childhood as morally redemptive, with adult men cared for and spiritually rehabilitated by children. Mean miserly Scrooge is saved by Tiny Tim, a crusty old earl by Little Lord Fauntleroy – 'such a beautiful, innocent little fellow he was too, with his brave, trustful face' – and Silas Marner, in a novel full of Wordsworthian resonances, by the girl Eppy:

> . . . .the little child had come to link him once more with the whole world. There was love between him and the child that blent them into one, and there was love between the child and the world. . . .

Another popular subject was the young girl in the guise of secular goddess, a theme favoured by Thomas Gotch in works such as *The Child Enthroned*, which took their style from Renaissance religious paintings. Behind them lay the feeling that innocent girlhood was a model for pure womanhood – a belief held passionately by Lewis Carroll. Taken to an extreme, it led to the fantasy of youth romantically preserved for ever in early death – the governing idea behind Henry Wallis's portrait of Chatterton, the poisoned young poet; drowned Ophelia, painted by Millais and by Arthur Hughes; Proserpine, Rossetti's girl-goddess of the Underworld, and the many soppy images of the infant as saint, bravely dying because he is too pure to live. Dickens perfected the child death scene, as in this from *The Old Curiosity Shop*:

> He was a very young boy; quite a little child. His hair still hung in curls about his face, and his eyes were very bright; but their light was of Heaven, not earth.

'Don't cry Papa', whispers William, 'raising his feeble hand caressingly to his father's cheek' in Mrs Henry Wood's *East Lynne*, a bestseller in 1861, 'I am not afraid to go, Jesus is coming for me.' A landmark in the cult of the pure dead child was the four volumes of the journal of a child who had died aged eight, Marjory Fleming (1803–11); they were published between 1858 and 1863, to popular acclaim. Later came Thomas Hardy's suicidal child Little Father Time ('Done because we are too many') and Marie Corelli's suicidal boy Lionel ('this world frightens me . . . but of You I am not afraid') in *The Mighty Atom*. A work painted within a few years of these two novels, George Elgar Hicks's *A Cloud with a Silver*

Lining, with its steely angel hovering overhead to pick off the soul of the dying baby, twins the child as sacrificial victim and spiritual king: in its echoes of both an Adoration and a *Pietà*, it expresses in one image the moral and psychological impetus behind the Victorian love affair with childhood.

What made these portrayals of childhood so popular and so powerful? It was not just the social and cultural climate; it was also the Victorian attitude to sexuality which inspired many of these images.

A clue to these attitudes, and to how they affected children's books, lies in the letters Lewis Carroll wrote to and about little girls. In 1892, two years after Hicks had painted *A Cloud with a Silver Lining*, the sixty-year-old Carroll addressed the mother of one of his child-friends. '*Many* thanks for again lending me Enid,' he said. 'She is one of the dearest of children. It is *good* for one (I mean, for one's spiritual life, and in the same sense in which reading the Bible is good) to come into contact with such sweetness and innocence.'[9] This has all the overtones of the morally redemptive vision of Little Lord Fauntleroy or Silas Marner, but in a personal context it does not ring quite true. It may be the effect of our post-Freudian age; it is also because it tells only half the story of Carroll's feelings. For other letters show how obsessive Carroll was in his search for little girl-friends; how he conducted these relationships like romances, and that one of his favourite hobbies was to photograph young girls naked. 'Would you kindly let me know what is the minimum amount of dress in which you are willing to have her taken?'[10] he wrote to a Mrs Chataway, whose daughter he had met on a seaside holiday. To Gertrude Chataway, aged nine, he beseeched, 'Explain to me how I am to enjoy Sandown without *you*. How can I walk on the beach alone? How can I sit alone on those wooden steps? So, you see, as I shan't be able to do without you, you will have to come. I send you seven kisses (to last a week).'[11]

Carroll was at once a nineteenth-century Humbert Humbert, driven by forbidden desires, drawing the guileless into his web, and a Victorian innocent who idolised childhood, remained at heart a child himself, and found in romance with little girls a release from social and moral pressures. In his Alice books, he celebrates a little girl, turns her into a Queen – when, as a pawn, she reaches the eighth square in *Through the Looking-Glass* – and reveres her innocence and simplicity. Yet those very qualities, in an age which often concealed or denied sexuality, made her desirable. The Alice books, like much that is great in Victorian art – Dickens's novels, Ruskin's prose, Rossetti's portraits – are romantic works moulded by sexual repression.

'People who were born too late to experience in boyhood and adolescence the intellectual and moral pressure of Victorianism have no idea of the fog and fetters which weighed one down', wrote Leonard Woolf in his autobiography. He was describing an age when Thomas Bowdler's edition of Shakespeare expurgated of sexual connotation was found in many civilised homes, when Gladstone referred publicly to the fifteen-year-old Prince of Wales kissing a girl on holiday as 'this squalid little debauch', when Mrs Gaskell, writing to fellow novelist George Eliot, who lived unmarried with G. H. Lewes, finished her letter, 'I should not be quite true in my ending, if I did not say before I concluded that I wish you *were* Mrs Lewes',[12] and when Queen Victoria refused to accept Mrs Millais at court because she had formerly, in an unconsummated marriage, been Mrs Ruskin. The restrictiveness created absurd double standards. Famous men visited George Eliot, but did not think it proper that their wives be introduced to her. Millais was welcomed at a garden party given by the Duke of Portland, while his wife walked across London to keep him company, then turned back at the door and returned home alone, an outcast among the English upper classes because of her sexual history. It also led to hypocrisy on sexual matters: Dickens, for example, maintained the public image of a virtuous and devoted family man while secretly keeping a mistress, whom he installed in a house in Slough and visited several times a week for thirteen years under the disguise of 'Mr Tringham'.

Behind this so-called morality was a reticence and suspicion about female desire, which was associated with loose or dangerous women, the *femmes fatales* of legend. Dickens's heroines are good girls who exhibit no sexual desires of their own; they die young and untainted, like Little Nell, or they become innocent child-brides like Amy Dorrit, whose much older husband 'took her in his arms, as if she had been his daughter'. For his celebration of female chastity, *The Golden Stair*, Edward Burne-Jones painted a procession of eighteen young virgins descending a staircase towards a door symbolising the threshold of their innocence; their faces are those of his upper- middle-class friends but he used the same working-class professional model for all the bodies – 'a perfect expression', says the critic Gay Daly, 'of Victorian society's attitude that ladies had only heads and that women were just mindless bodies'.[13] That this was a particularly English trait is suggested by the comparison between the mature, worldly women trumpeted in nineteenth-century European art – Anna Karenina, Carmen, Manet's Olympia – and the pure little girls of Victorian culture – Dickens's heroines, Little Buttercup, the smock-frocked girls in playgrounds drawn by Kate Greenaway – among whom Alice in Wonderland belongs. Even 'fallen' women in English novels are innocent and unknowing victims, like Tess of the d'Urbervilles or Mrs Gaskell's Ruth, where their foreign counterparts are passionate schemers with their own desires such as Madame Bovary or Manon Lescaut.

But sex, when swept under the carpet, resurfaced in a potent and twisted form. In a society which refused to accept mature sexuality, and where even married women – Mrs Ruskin, Mrs Carlyle, Mrs Barrie – languished as virgins because their husbands declined sexual involvement, the pre-sexual child became an obvious ideal. Because women's sexuality was most strongly denied, the pre-sexual girl, the epitome of innocent beauty which awakens longing without itself demanding sexual satisfaction, was above all idealised. And as inevitably, adult sexual desires which were discouraged and distrusted were subconsciously redirected towards children, because in the context of a pre-sexual child they were sufficiently taboo to seem safe, unchallenging and hardly sexual at all – a fantasy which could be feverishly imagined but never realised, a focus for emotional satisfaction which never threatened the ideal of chastity.

The mix of hypocrisy, innocence and voyeurism which marks Victorian sexual attitudes to children and young girls has its roots in these not-quite-admitted yet intensely dreamed fantasies. The mix enabled Lewis Carroll to plan to bowdlerise Bowdler and produce an even cleaner edition of Shakespeare for young women at the same time as he photographed little girls naked in his rooms at Christ Church. It enabled both Gladstone and Dickens to indulge an obsession with young prostitutes, to stalk them as they walked the London streets at night and to listen to their histories, all the while telling themselves that Christian reform and charity, rather than personal titillation, was their motive.

As the moral climate encouraged the submerging of sexual feelings into a spiritual ideal, the two became inextricably mixed together. 'Bursting out like one of the sweet Surrey fountains, all dazzling and pure, you have the radiance and innocence of reinstated infant divinity showered again among the flowers of English meadows,' Ruskin said of Kate Greenaway's pictures at an Oxford lecture in 1883. Privately, he found this 'divinity' so sensual that he became almost addicted to her drawings, asking her to send him more and more, and of girls wearing less and less. 'Will you,' he begged Greenaway in a letter written the same year as the Oxford lecture, ' – (it's all for your own good –!) make her stand up and then draw her for me without a cap – and, without her shoes – (because of the heels) and without her mittens, and without her – frock and frills? And let me see exactly how tall she is – and – how – round. It will be so good of and for you – And to and for me.'[14]

It is no coincidence that the two great male novelists of the period, Dickens and Hardy, created male characters unable to come to terms with adult female sexuality but strongly drawn to little girl types – hence the tragedies of David Copperfield and his child-wife Dora, and of Angel Clare and Tess of the d'Urbervilles, whom he repudiates when she turns out not to be the child-bride of his dreams. Even the virile Mr Rochester talks of Jane Eyre during his courtship in the coy terms of Fairyland: 'it was a fairy, and come from Elf-land . . . a little thing with a veil of gossamer on its head'. And the bachelor scholar hemmed in by repressions and fears of sex is a common Victorian character – Charlotte Bronte's St John Rivers, George Eliot's Casaubon, Hardy's Angel and Jude. He seems to have reflected a social trend. 'There were by modern standards . . . large numbers of unmarried men in nineteenth century England', says Michael Mason in *The Making of Victorian Sexuality*, 'and it is quite likely that nineteenth century bachelors . . . actively declined to marry.'[15] Among the fantasy writers, Lewis Carroll and Edward Lear certainly made that choice; J. M. Barrie lived as a bachelor even when married; Kenneth Grahame married late, reluctantly and disastrously. All turned their emotional energies to children or childish pursuits in ways which fitted the culture of a time when celibacy was far more socially acceptable than it is today.

Children's books, and stories in which children have emotionally and spiritually significant roles, then, emerged from the Victorian cult of childhood and innocence, and were directly influenced by cultural reticence about sex and desire. In this context, the sexual undercurrents in the English books written for children in the 1850s–70s are of interest. Christina Rossetti's *Speaking Likenesses* (1874), for example, has a party of distorted children where the boys are studded with quills and hooks and the girls are slithery and slimy – an image seething with sexuality:

> One boy bristled with prickly quills like a porcupine, and raised or depressed them at pleasure; but he usually kept them pointed outwards. Another instead of being rounded like most people was facetted at very sharp angles. A third caught in everything he came near, for he was hung round with hooks like fishhooks. One girl

exuded a sticky fluid and came off on the fingers; another, rather smaller, was slimy and slipped through the hands.

Charles Kingsley, the writer-theologian who recommended regimes of abstinence and flagellation to his fiancée Fanny, delayed consummation after marriage for a month, apparently to heighten excitement, and sent Fanny pictures of the two of them as lovers indulging in bondage sex on a cross, created in *The Water Babies* (1863) a tale riddled with images of sexual guilt and contamination. His theme came from Blake's poem 'The Chimney Sweeper', where a sweep dreams he is:

> . . . lock'd up in coffins of black.
> And by came an Angel, who had a bright key,
> And he open'd the coffins and set them all free;
> Then down a green plain leaping, laughing, they run,
> And wash in a river, and shine in the Sun.

Kingsley adopted the Romantic country/city, heaven/hell imagery, but added a moral-sexual layer. His sweep Tom screams for regeneration from his sooty, town-soiled self as he plunges into a country stream with the cry 'I want to be clean!', but he must cleanse himself morally, of his wicked thoughts, before he can be a fit companion for the heroine Ellie, a pure, white, chaste Victorian miss. Ruskin, in *The King of the Golden River* (1851), the tale of a river valley destroyed by human corruption and redeemed by a pure asexual child who becomes its king, uses similar imagery.

Nothing in Lear's poems or the Alice books is as unsubtle or as moralistic as this. Most of the early fantasies, however, employ images which call attention to a sense of psychological release. *Alice's Adventures in Wonderland* opens in a pool of tears. Edward Lear's characters – the Owl and the Pussy Cat, the Daddy Long-legs and the Fly, the Jumblies – sail away to sea and freedom. *The Water Babies* begins with a plunge into the river. And when in George MacDonald's *The Light Princess* (1867), the story of a girl whose attitude to life is so lightweight that she literally floats, the heroine finally ceases to keep emotion at bay and bursts into tears, it is as if a whole layer of Victorian repression of feeling is peeled back in an image which epitomises the breakthrough of fantasy: 'all the pent-up crying of her life was spent now'.

Today, most of these books seem wooden and dated, Victorian museum pieces; only Carroll's and Lear's works are now widely read. To see Carroll and Lear in the context of their contemporaries, however, is to understand some of the social and psychological factors which drew them to fantasy. For, as a safely unreal and child-centred mode of writing, fantasy allowed an unbuttoning of the psyche for men who felt oppressed by Victorian propriety and restraint. In fantasy, unconscious or repressed desires could be expressed, and this is why strict and sombre Victorian England inspired so great an outburst of anarchic, escapist, nonsensical children's books.

A chief pleasure in both Lear's poems and the Alice books is that they celebrate rebellion and chaos, point no morals, rejoice in freewheeling thought. That liberty, however, is framed and made possible by their concentration on child and child-like characters, and on an audience of children which, as Carroll's epilogue to *Alice's Adventures in Wonderland* makes clear, was thought to be better, purer, more imaginative, than adults:

> Lastly, she pictured to herself how this same little sister of hers would, in the after-time, be herself a grown woman; and how she would keep, through all her riper years, the simple and loving heart of her childhood; and how she would gather about her other little children, and make *their* eyes bright and eager with many a strange tale . . . and how she would feel with all their simple sorrows, and find a pleasure in all their simple joys, remembering her own child-life, and the happy summer days.

The tone of such an emphasis on childhood prepared the way for the view, which gained ground in late Victorian England, that only youth mattered. That sentiment had a profound effect on J. M. Barrie and Kenneth Grahame, and will be discussed in Chapters Four and Five. It was an idea given voice by A. E. Housman, in the youthful martyrs of *A*

Shropshire Lad, 'the lads who will die in their glory and never be old', and by Oscar Wilde in his depiction of Dorian Gray, to whom eternal youth was the goal of life, and it created the mood for the Nineties dandy. 'I am in mourning for my birthday', Wilde used to lament each year. In 1888 he published a volume of fairy tales, *The Happy Prince*, in which immortal youth reigns triumphant: in one story a child leads a giant to Paradise by showing him how to play and to love, and in another the golden statue of a young prince, a typical Wildean golden boy, transcends the petty bourgeois society which torments him and lives for ever in Heaven.

The volume marks the transition between the Victorian view of children, which idealised their virtue and innocence, and the *fin de siècle* and Edwardian celebration of youth for youthful pleasure's sake. In Grahame's *The Wind in the Willows* (1908) a group of animals, much like boys, mess about in boats, picnic and party – the book is a homage to the playfulness that dominated Edwardian culture. In *Peter Pan* (1904), the story of a boy who remains always young, Barrie expressed the feelings and aspirations of a society which did not want to grow up.

Peter Pan is a direct descendant of Alice in Wonderland. From Carroll's ideal of pure little girls in the 1860s, through Barrie's dream of ever-young boys in the 1900s, and then to Milne's 1920s nostalgia for a youthful, untroubled world, we can see the evolution of an image. The vision of childhood in English culture developed with the changing social climate, renewing itself to remain a powerful influence on literature and art for seventy years. How it worked on the creative imaginations of children's fantasy writers is the subject of the following chapters.

2

Lewis Carroll:
the Child as Muse

'And just as I'd taken the highest tree in the wood,' continued the Pigeon, raising its voice to a shriek, 'and just as I was thinking I should be free of them at last, they must needs come wriggling down from the sky! Ugh, Serpent!'

'But I'm *not* a serpent, I tell you!' said Alice. 'I'm a – I'm a –'

'Well! *What* are you?' said the Pigeon. 'I can see you're trying to invent something!'

'I – I'm a little girl,' said Alice, rather doubtfully. . . .

Lewis Carroll,
Alice's Adventures in Wonderland

Lewis Carroll was born Charles Lutwidge Dodgson in 1832, the first son in a large, warm and close family which included many sisters and maiden aunts. His father, Archdeacon Charles Dodgson, was a parson in the Cheshire village of Daresbury, outside Warrington; later his fortunes rose and he became rector at Croft, an affluent resort town on the river Tees near Darlington. As a young boy 'Charlie' was educated in a cosy, rambling parsonage by kind, devout and learned parents who poured all their energies into their children. He was precocious, adored mathematics and drawing, built a toy theatre and marionettes, and liked dressing up in a white gown and brown wig to perform conjuring tricks and puppet shows for his sisters. From his father, he developed an early love of nonsense. A letter from Archdeacon Dodgson, away in Leeds, to his eight-year-old son, for example, reads:

> Then what a bawling & a tearing of hair there will be! Pigs and babies, camels and Butterflies, rolling in the gutter together – old women rushing up chimnies & cows after them – ducks hiding themselves in coffee cups and fat geese trying to squeeze themselves into pencil cases – at last the Mayor of Leeds will be found in a soup plate covered up with custard & stuck full of almonds to make him look like a sponge cake that he may escape the dreadful destruction of the town.[1]

The germ of the Alice books, with their babies turning into pigs, bread-and-butterflies, little girls stuck in chimneys, talking puddings and people leaping into soup tureens, is here, and soon Carroll began to compose his own nonsense. At twelve he wrote a mocking poem about turning a sister into mutton broth which ends 'Never stew your sister'; to his younger brother Skeffington he sent a letter warning, 'Roar not lest thou be abolished.'

As a boy, Carroll poured nonsense verses into two family magazines, 'Useful and Instructive Poetry' and 'The Rectory Magazine', which he produced to amuse his sisters. Like his magic tricks, they show him already engaged in the favourite pastime which endured all his life: entertaining little girls. Here he was confident, an exhibitionist, able to give his talents full reign. Beyond home, however, he became withdrawn, awkward, self-conscious, and he stammered. His few years at Rugby were miserable and lonely, although he was clever, hard-working and always came home with prizes. But he spent a perfect final year of childhood studying at home, mostly in the rectory garden, while being cossetted by his mother and sisters. Mrs Dodgson, watching her family at this time, spoke of 'the responsibility incurred by a lot of so much happiness . . . that it really at times was alarming to look round her & feel that she had not a wish unfulfilled'.[2] It was from this family haven that Carroll went up to Christ Church, Oxford, in 1851.

Two days after he arrived, the idyll was broken. His mother, aged forty-seven, died suddenly, leaving a dependent and adoring family of eleven children, nearly all under twenty, numb with grief and shock. For Carroll, the first to leave home, her death marked the end of a blissful youth which he always recalled as a golden age; by twenty-one, childhood was crystallised in his imagination as an ideal state, and he wrote his sentimental farewell to it:

> I'd give all wealth that years have piled,
>   The slow result of Life's decay,
> To be once more a little child
>   For one bright summer-day.

At Christ Church, Carroll grew into an adult version of the shy, stuttering, sensitive and gifted scholar of the Rugby years. Oxford was the natural spiritual home of such a type, and a successful career as undergraduate and fellow, backed by his father's Anglican connections, was more or less predetermined for him. He worked hard, attended chapel, conformed to the social and academic norms of the college, and graduated with a first in mathematics. As a logician, the intellectual fastidiousness which later marked the Alice books began to show itself: in an early paper, for example, he pointed out that a stopped clock is more accurate than one that loses a minute a day – the first clock is exactly right every twenty-four hours, the other once every two years. 'Can you keep from crying by considering things?' asks Alice in *Through the Looking-Glass*. With single-minded rigour, Carroll channelled his emotions into work, and his passion for order now extended to every aspect of his life.

It was as a young graduate at Christ Church that he began to keep meticulous diaries, to file and index every letter he ever received, and to record the menu offered to every guest entertained in his rooms. He was fussy, prim, zealous and tough on himself. In his diary he lists his faults as 'failing to clear arrears of lecture work every evening' and 'indulging in sleep in the evening'. 'I pray God to help me to begin a life of more regular and better habits'[3] is a frequent refrain; overhearing 'a painful amount of open jesting and flippancy on sacred topics'[4] is a typical complaint. Expressions of emotion are rare, and his reaction to the stormy passion of *Wuthering Heights* – 'it is of all novels I ever read the one I should least like to be a character in myself. All the "dramatis personae" are so unusual and unpleasant'[5] – suggests a horror of feelings beyond his control.

His personal life was run on strictly logical and disciplined lines. He tested his nerve and stamina by watching an hour-long amputation of a leg at St Bartholomew's Hospital, because 'this is an experiment I have long been anxious to make, in order to know whether I might rely on myself to be of any use in cases of emergency, and I am very glad to believe that I might'.[6] He was not quite one of those Victorians whose morning swim broke the ice on the river Cherwell, but he kept fit by taking regular eighteen-mile walks, timed to take five hours and twenty-five minutes and average three and three-quarter miles an hour. He was abstemious, unseduced by the luxuries of High Table, and remained thin as a stick all his life. Although he became wine-taster to the college, he believed the fellows over-indulged, and was always shocked when his child-guests evinced healthy appetites. In the Alice books, food is a terror and an indulgence: a baby is tormented by pepper, the dormouse by a teapot, Alice is almost assaulted by a soup ladle. Tyrants exhibit gastronomic excess, from the Hatter's 'I eat what I see' to the Walrus and the Carpenter gobbling up all their oyster-companions. Carroll prefers the refined tastes he hoped little girls would have: the sisters who eat only treacle, the bread-and-butterfly living on weak tea.

The terror and indulgence of food at the mad tea-party in *Alice's Adventures in Wonderland*: 'The table was a large one, but the three were all crowded together at one corner of it: "No room! No room!" they cried when they saw Alice coming. "There's plenty of room!" said Alice indignantly, and she sat down in a large arm-chair at one end of the table.'

In photographs from this time, Carroll is a handsome, stiff young man: his lean, asymmetrical face, with its nervous look, gentle eyes and intelligent, twisted smile, is framed by neatly coiffured dark curling hair. He is always formally dressed, often in a top hat, and with white gloves in summer; his posture is taut and erect – Alice Liddell, the model for the Alice books, said later that he 'carried himself upright, almost more than upright, as if he had swallowed a poker'[7] – and his expression reveals neither happiness nor sadness. His fast, jerky gait was known in Oxford; the photographs suggest pent-up energy and intense self-control. Contemporaries saw him as a quiet conformist; he did not easily form close friendships, and was known as a loner. 'We all,' recorded a Christ Church under-graduate, 'sat in the same hall and some of us even at the same table with Dodgson without discovering . . . the wit, the peculiar humour, that was in him. We looked upon him as a rising mathematician, nothing more. He seldom spoke, and the slight impediment in his speech was not conducive to conver-sation.'[8] It was not conducive to good teaching either, and undergraduates remembered Carroll as a remote, humourless figure whose lectures were notoriously tedious; Carroll, intel-lectually aloof, in turn found them dull, while a spell of school-teaching was harrowing and confirmed a life-long dislike of little boys. 'Boys are not in my line,' he once said. 'I think they are a mistake'.[9]

Yet his cleverness and orderly ways were noticed and approved, and he was nominated for a Studentship at Christ Church by Oxford's controversial High Churchman, Dr Pusey, Regius Professor of Hebrew and an old family friend. The post, like many nineteenth-century academic awards, required the recipient to take holy orders and not to marry; those who did forfeited the job, though alternative livings were often found. But Pusey, wrote a contemporary, 'made an idol of celibacy . . . no woman was safe except in a nunnery, no man except in orders', and for him 'if only the youth were pious, earnest, docile, the great thing was to fix, to secure, to *capture* him'.[10] Carroll was Pusey's man. A fellow at twenty-three, he was caught within the solitary, elitist life of college and church; at twenty-nine he was ordained deacon, and he remained a bachelor don at Oxford until his death almost half a century later. He kept the same rooms for thirty years, never married, travelled abroad once, spent his holidays at the English seaside, cared for his sisters, and when he died in 1898 was the blameless subject of a starry biography written by his nephew.

'If Oxford dons in the nineteenth century had an essence, he was that essence,' wrote Virginia Woolf. 'He was so good that his sisters worshipped him; so pure that his nephew had nothing to say about him . . . But this untinted jelly contained within it a perfectly hard crystal. It contained childhood . . . It lodged in him whole and entire.' Beneath the conventional Oxford existence was an intense private world which centred on little girls, with whom his shyness and stammer vanished immediately, and whom he collected obsessively and desperately as friends and correspondents, at social gatherings, on trains, at the beach, in college, from his twenties until his death.

At the seaside, for example, he carried a black bag full of toys and gifts to woo little girls, plus a supply of safety pins to hitch up the skirts of those who agreed to paddle in the surf. One, who fell in the water, was accosted by Carroll with a piece of blotting paper and the greeting, 'May I offer you this to blot yourself with?' He invented travelling games, boards with pegs and figures, wire puzzles, which he took on train journeys as weapons of conquest. He judged the success of his annual seaside holiday by the number of girl-friends made, and travelled up and down the country to renew the most promising contacts. There was no question of casual acquaintances picked up and dropped. To a mother he wrote: 'Would you kindly tell me if I may reckon your girls as invitable . . . to tea, or dinner, *singly*. I know of cases where they are invitable in *sets* only (like the circulating library novels), and such friendships I don't think worth going on with. I don't think anyone knows what girl-nature *is*, who has only seen them in the presence of their mother or sisters.'[11]

Carroll's rooms at Christ Church were in part a nursery, housing music-boxes, dolls, puzzles, wind-up animals including a walking bear and 'Bob the Bat', who flew around the room. When he entertained a child-friend there, or caught a glimpse of a particularly beautiful little girl, he wrote in his diary, 'I mark this day with a white stone'. One of the most talented of the early Victorian photographers, he catalogued little girls among his acquaintance who might be photographed, listing them by Christian name and date of birth. The progression of his photographs unravels like the sexuality lurking behind Victorian sentimentality. At first he took children in fairy-tale poses such as Agnes Weld, Tennyson's niece, as Little Red Riding Hood, in a fine photo of 1852 shown in a London exhibition, or in mawkish guises such as the famous picture of Alice Liddell as a Beggar Child; eventually he moved on to the photos he referred to in his diary as 'sans habilement', and which he ordered to be destroyed after his death. So keen was he on these shots that he tried to barter with mothers for them. 'Now don't crush all my hopes,' he wrote to a Mrs Mayhew, whom he approached after meeting her husband, the Hebrew Lecturer at Wadham College, and hearing that the couple had pretty daughters:

> At *any* rate, I trust you will let me do some pictures of *Janet* naked; at her age, it seems almost absurd to even suggest any scruple about dress.
>
> My great hope, I confess, is about *Ethel* . . . Do consider *her* case in reference to the fact that she herself is quite indifferent about dress.
>
> If the worst comes to the worst, and you won't concede any nudities at all, I think you ought to allow *all three* to be done in bathing-drawers, to make up for my disappointment!
>
> P.S. . . . what I like best of all is to have *two* hours of leisure-time before me, *one* child to photograph, and *no* restrictions as to costume! (It is a descending Arithmetical Series – 2, 1, 0.)[12]

The wonder was not that Mrs Mayhew said no, but that so many Victorian mothers receiving similar requests said yes; some even promised, when Carroll beseeched them, to arrange introductions to other families with beautiful girls.

In Oxford, he was something of a Pied Piper figure; Ethel Arnold, grand-daughter of Thomas Arnold of Rugby and niece of Matthew Arnold, recalled the pandemonium that broke out when a group of children and their governesses met Carroll in the street in Oxford and formed a chain to prevent him passing:

> The line broke in confusion, and the next moment four of the little band were clinging to such portions of the black-coated figure as they could seize upon. Two little people, however, hung back, being seized with shyness and a sudden consciousness of their audacity, a sudden awe of this tall dignified gentleman in black broadcloth and white tie. But in a moment he had shaken off the clinging, laughing children, and before the two little strangers had time to realize what had happened, they found themselves trotting along on either side of him, a hand of each firmly clasped in the strong, kind hands of Lewis Carroll, and chatting away as if they had known him all their lives.[13]

Gertrude Chataway, one of his favourite child-friends, recalled being 'a little girl about 8½ absolutely entranced with the lodger next door'[14] on holiday at Sandown, and running out on to her balcony to see him every time he went out on to his to 'sniff' the sea air.

That he was a huge success with little girls is indisputable. Yet in a post-Freudian age it is almost impossible to read the thousands of letters he wrote to them without detecting a secret sensuality – the one, for example, where he imagines taking tea with Gertrude Chataway, who cries:

> Boo! hoo! Here's Mr Dodgson has drunk my health; and I haven't got any left!

while her mother, in an imaginary visit to the doctor, explains:

> You see she *would* go and make friends with a strange gentleman, and yesterday he drank her health.[15]

And in a subsequent letter to Gertrude, he imagines his own trip to the doctor to cure his sore lips:

> 'I think you must have been giving too many kisses.'
> 'Well,' I said, 'I did give *one* kiss to a baby child, a little

friend of mine.' 'Think again,' he said, 'are you sure it was only *one*?' I thought again, and said, 'Perhaps it was eleven times.' Then the Doctor said, 'You must not give her *any* more till your lips are quite rested again.' 'But what am I to do?' I said, 'because, you see, I owe her 182 more.'[16]

The emotion he poured into these friendships is terrifying in its intensity, its underlying sense of loss, its one-sidedness. Agnes Hull, whom he met on holiday at Eastbourne, received a flood of letters addressed to 'my darling Aggie' which joke flirtatiously at Carroll's disappointment:

Oh yes, I know quite well what you're saying – 'Why ca'n't the man take a *hint*? He might have *seen* that the beginning of my last letter was meant to show that my affection was cooling down!' Why, of course I saw it! But is that any reason why *mine* should cool down, to match? . . . haven't I a right to be affectionate if I like?[17]

To another girl just met on the beach, he wrote:

Oh child, child! I kept my promise yesterday afternoon, and came down to the sea, to go with you along the rocks, but I saw you going with another gentleman, so I thought I wasn't wanted just yet: so I walked a bit, and when I got back, I couldn't see you anywhere, though I went a good way on the rocks to look. There *was* a child in pink that looked you: but when I got up to her, it was the wrong child: however, that wasn't her fault, poor thing. . . . So I helped her with her sandcastles and then I went home. I didn't cry *all* the way.[18]

In every letter he penned to little girls, sadness co-exists with relief in pouring out his longings; he is the suitor who expects rejection because he knows his quest can go nowhere, that the little girls will grow up and find him silly and he will have to catch new child-friends, over and over again. He mentions giving a child presents in exchange for smiling when she met him in the street and for pretending to be amused at his jokes. 'Don't grow a bit older,' he tells Gertrude Chataway in a letter which recalls Alice growing smaller and larger by turns, 'for I shall want to take you in the same dress again: if anything, you'd better grow a *little* younger – go back to your last birthday but one.'[19]

Carroll was adamant that in these friendships he was above reproach, holding the Victorian view that contact with children was morally uplifting. 'I have been largely privileged in tête-à-tête intercourse with children,' he said at the end of his life. 'It is very healthy and helpful to one's own spiritual life: and humbling too, to come into contact with souls so much purer, and nearer to God, than one feels oneself to be.'[20] He was always open about his child-friends and proper in requesting leave from parents to see them. In his sixties he was still asking a mother whether her daughter, visiting the Carroll family home, could sit alone with him in his sitting room rather than be restricted to his sisters' drawing room. There is no evidence that he sought physical contact beyond a kiss or a hand to hold, or that he wanted any form of sexual fulfilment. Much of his feeling was Victorian sentiment blown up into an obsession, as is suggested by the admission to a young friend that 'when I get letters signed "your loving", I always *kiss* the signature. You see I'm a sentimental old fogey!'[21] 'I have imagined so much, and had so little,' said another great nineteenth-century children's writer, Hans Christian Andersen. The same was true of Carroll's emotional life, lived so acutely in fantasy and so barren in fact.

'My mental picture is as vivid as ever, of one who was, through so many years, my ideal child-friend. I have had scores of child-friends since your time; but they have been quite a different thing,'[22] Carroll wrote to Alice Liddell twenty years after *Alice's Adventures in Wonderland* was published. He first saw her in 1855, when she was three years old and her father, Henry Liddell, became Dean of Christ Church. The same year, Carroll was appointed a fellow of the college; at twenty-three he was a shy, promising mathematician who had little to do with the imposing and aristocratic dean, and still kept one foot in the world of his sisters and 'The Rectory Magazine'. That year, he wrote for them a 'stanza of Anglo-Saxon poetry' which was to become one of the most famous of all nonsense rhymes:

> Twas brillig, and the slithy toves
>   Did gyre and gimble in the wabe:
> All mimsy were the borogoves,
>   And the mome raths outgrabe.

It was not published immediately, but Carroll did begin sending contributions to a periodical called *Comic Times* and to its successor *The Train*. He insisted on a pseudonym, offering Edgar Cuthwellis ('made by a transposition out of Charles Lutwidge') or Lewis Carroll ('derived from Lutwidge . . . Ludovic . . . Louis, and Charles'). On 1 March 1856 he recorded 'Lewis Carroll chosen'. A week later, he was invited to a soirée at the deanery, and made friends with Liddell's oldest daughter, six-year-old Lorina. Within a month, he was watching out for all the Dean's children, three pretty little girls and a boy, from the windows of Christ Church library. Mrs Liddell allowed him to photograph them, and he struck up a special rapport with Alice. 'The three little girls were in the garden most of the time, and we became excellent friends: we tried to group them in the foreground of the picture, but they were not patient sitters. I mark this day with a stone,' he wrote in April 1856. He had already become Lewis Carroll; everything was set for *Alice's Adventures in Wonderland*.

The genesis of the Alice books is a well-known story. On the afternoon of 4 July 1862, Lewis Carroll, his friend Robinson Duckworth, a fellow at Trinity, in straw boaters and white flannel trousers, and Lorina, Alice and Edith Liddell, aged thirteen, ten and eight, in white cotton dresses and big-brimmed hats, crossed Christ Church Meadow to Folly Bridge, picked a boat, rowed three miles upstream to Godstow, unpacked their picnic hamper and did not return to the deanery until nine o'clock. The story, Duckworth recounted, 'was actually composed and spoken over my shoulder for the benefit of Alice Liddell, who was acting as "cox" of our gig. I remember turning round and saying, "Dodgson, is this an extempore romance of yours?" And he replied, "Yes, I'm inventing as we go along." '23

Carroll later recalled the beginning of the book as an afternoon in paradise:

> Full many a year has slipped away, since that 'golden afternoon' that gave thee birth, but I can call it up almost as clearly as if it were yesterday – the cloudless blue above, the watery mirror below, the boat drifting idly on its way, the tinkle of the drops that fell from the oars, as they waved so sleepily to and fro, and (the one bright gleam of life in all the slumberous scene) the three eager faces, hungry for news of fairyland, and who would not be said 'nay' to: from whose lips 'Tell us a story, please,' had all the stern immutability of Fate!

'In a desperate attempt to strike out some new line of fairy lore,' Carroll continued, he sent Alice 'straight down a rabbit hole . . . without the least idea what was to happen afterwards'.[24] He included all the passengers in the boat – Alice the favourite as herself, Lorina as the lory, Edith as the eaglet, Duckworth as the duck and Carroll-Dodgson as the do-do, a reference to the stutter with which he introduced himself as 'Do-Do-Dodgson'. Later, the girls reappear as the delicate sisters who lived on treacle, Elsie (LC, from the initials Lorina Charlotte), Lacie (an anagram of Alice) and Tillie (from Edith's nickname Matilda). Alice loved the story, and when they returned to Christ Church, she said 'Oh Mr Dodgson, I wish you would write out Alice's Adventures for me', and Carroll stayed up through the night to begin the book.

Carroll's friendship with Alice Liddell was the most intense relationship he knew, and into the books she inspired he poured all the hopes and longings, the frustrations and anxieties, for which he had no other expression. That the Alice books were a joy to write, a creative thrill, is obvious from every line and every character; as clear is the rage and pain which came hand-in-hand with Carroll's sudden unleashing of imagination and emotion.

In inventing Wonderland as a beautiful, child-centred

universe set apart from adult life, Carroll drew on memories of his childhood garden at Croft Rectory, on the view of the Liddell girls playing in the deanery garden which he saw each day from his Christ Church window, and, probably unconsciously, on one of the oldest traditions in literature – the perfect place, the Eden of Christianity, the exquisite rose garden which has captured the artistic imagination from courtly medieval poetry such as *The Romance of the Rose* to Eliot's *Burnt Norton*.

All this dovetailed with the sense of fun and nonsense which had been part of his childhood, and with his love of mathematics and logic. Wonderland, therefore, took its character from the distorted, intellectual nonsense perspectives – the Cheshire Cat who leaves its grin behind, the Mock Turtle who was once a real turtle – unique to Carroll the poet-don, and it is thus at once an exciting, new, topsy-turvy world and an age-old, mythic place. It has, for example, the serpent of Eden – but only in the comic imagination of a hysterical character, the Pigeon, who mistakes Alice for a snake. It has the secret, desirable rose garden, but when Alice gets there it is a joke, a scene out of a child's colouring book: Alice unlocks the door with a golden key:

> . . . and *then* – she found herself at last in the beautiful garden, among the bright flower-beds and the cool fountains.
>
> A large rose-tree stood near the entrance of the garden: the roses growing on it were white, but there were three gardeners at it, busily painting them red . . . 'Why, the fact is, you see, Miss, this here ought to have been a *red* rose-tree, and we put a white one in by mistake; and, if the Queen was to find out, we should all have our heads cut off, you know.'

And so two traditions meet: the idea of an escapist Paradise, with its resonance of lost innocence and unattainability, and the comic, anarchic spirit of nonsense, with its roots in English nursery rhymes.

Through nonsense, Carroll responded in *Alice's Adventures*

in Wonderland and *Through the Looking-Glass* to the turbulent and changing Victorian world. Fantasy, eccentricity, any sort of weird inventiveness, were part of the fabric of nineteenth-century England. Victorians opening their morning newspapers and reading of the invention of photography, say, or of a massive venture like the building of the British Museum, might, like the White Queen, be expected to believe 'as many as six impossible things before breakfast'. In the nonsense of the Alice books, Carroll distilled trends and characteristics which were part of everyday life.

The Red Queen, running faster and faster to stay in the same place, is the quintessence of the frenetic, ambitious capitalist in the new industrial England. The prehistoric menagerie which opens *Alice* suggests the excitement and fear caused by the new theories of evolution – Carroll was writing in Oxford just after the famous Oxford debate on evolution in 1860, where Bishop Wilberforce accused T. H. Huxley of being related to a monkey. Both the Alice books have comic, speeded-up reversals of evolution when a baby changes into a pig and a duchess

The fantasy railway carriage: 'A Goat, that was sitting next to the gentleman in white, shut his eyes and said in a loud voice, "She ought to know her way to the ticket-office, even if she doesn't know her alphabet!" '

becomes a sheep. And the monstrous, jumping train with a mind of its own, leaping through the air to cross a brook in *Through the Looking-Glass*, reflects Victorian terror at the power of the new steam engines which ran like rockets and ate up the countryside with their rails: 'The man that drives the engine. Why, the smoke alone is worth a thousand pounds a puff!'

Our own fantasy images in children's culture – space travel as epitomised by *ET*, the aggressive urban underworld of the Ninja Turtles, supposed to live in New York's sewers – reflect the preoccupations of the late twentieth century. In the same way nonsense literature charts the fear of meaninglessness which bubbles below the surface of Victorian culture, with its terror of godlessness and anarchy, and it does so by distorting and exaggerating precisely those new ideas and images which most shocked and disturbed the contemporary worldview.

Some of the most nonsensical characters and scenarios resemble people and events that the Liddell children would have known. The dormouse, for example, was based on Dante Gabriel Rossetti's pet wombat, which used to sleep on the table when guests, including Carroll, visited Rossetti at his Oxford home for tea. The Mad Hatter was modelled on a Christ Church servant turned furniture dealer called Theophilus Carter, known as the Mad Hatter because he always wore a top hat and had eccentric ideas, including the invention of an 'alarm clock bed', which woke the sleeper by throwing him out on to the floor, and which Carter exhibited at the Great Exhibition in 1851. The Hatter's preoccupations in the book are waking the dormouse, time and clocks, and furniture. In the upside-down milieu of nonsense, Carroll took to absurdist extremes aspects of Victorian intellectual, practical and emotional life.

How close parts of Carroll's fantasy came to Victorian reality is suggested in Stanley Weintraub's biography of Queen Victoria, which takes as an epigraph the Queen of Hearts's statement, 'I don't know what you mean by *your* way. All the ways round here belong to me' as personifying Victoria's autocratic and fanciful behaviour. Some scenes from Victoria's life read as though they come from the Alice books. Ceremonial dinners, for example, were cleared away, while guests were still eating, the instant the Queen, who was served first and ate fast, had finished her portion, leaving visiting aristocrats hungry and humiliated. When arguments were not going her way, Victoria flirted with madness, clutching her head and crying 'my reason! my reason!' The Queen was haughtily remote from her subjects, never read a newspaper, opposed reform, and rigorously supported social hierarchies. She was so pompous that her son, Edward VII, joked that she was reluctant to go to heaven because 'there the angels would precede her'.

Lewis Carroll was a fervent admirer of the Queen, a clergyman ordained in the Church of England, an Oxford academic and outwardly a man of the most conventional propriety – he once wrote to *The Times* to complain about the unseemly flippancy displayed towards curates in a W. S. Gilbert play. Yet he also suffered from the sobriety and restraint of nineteenth-century society. The Victorian children's hymn 'All Things Bright and Beautiful' with its rousing reinforcement of class hierarchy – 'The rich man in his castle/ The poor man at his gate/God made them, high or lowly/And ordered their estate' – expresses the intense veneration for order during the period. Carroll disciplined his emotional self almost into non-existence, and was pious and dutiful as a deacon at Christ Church, but beneath the surface was a passionate romantic, sexually frustrated and vengeful towards a world he saw as absurd. Just occasionally there is a clue to the stress in his letters. 'I should have no pleasure in doing any such pictures, now that I know I am ~~not thought fit for~~ only permitted such a privilege ~~except~~ on condition of being under chaperonage',[25] runs a reply to one mother, the words crossed out revealing his anxiety about how he was perceived. Like Edward Lear, the other great nonsense writer, he was an intense, buttoned-up loner whom a repressive society pushed into real eccentricity. Fantasy was his escape, a means of self-expression, a chance to reduce to chaos some of the establishment values – the law ('Sentence first – verdict afterwards'), education (reeling and writing) – which publicly he upheld.

In this context, it is worth looking at the Alice books as part of the genre of other mid-nineteenth-century children's fantasies. Most are claustrophobic, oppressive, jabbing in tone. *Alice* is a nightmare of violent but homely chaos. A flurry of watches and waistcoats and jars of marmalade opens the book, a dormouse is stuffed into a teapot, a cook throws saucepans and plates at a baby. The centrepiece of Christina Rossetti's *Speaking Likenesses* is a vicious birthday party of grotesque children who hurl missiles across the table and stab and hook each other with fishhooks. In George MacDonald's *The Light Princess*, the heroine wants to be tied to the sky and flown like a kite while it rains rose-water, hails sugar plums and snows whipped cream. And Edward Lear's verses are full of domestic props like the Yonghy Bonghy Bò's 'two old chairs, and half a candle/One old jug without a handle' or characters such as the Nutcrackers and the Sugar Tongs who escape domesticity while:

> The Spoons with a clatter looked out of the lattice,
> The Mustard-pot climbed up the Gooseberry Pies,
> The Soup-ladle peeped through a heap of Veal Patties,
> And squeaked with a ladle-like scream of surprise.

Victorian fantasy conjures up dark interiors, the cluttered kitchen and the over-decorated parlour, bric-à-brac and potted ferns and lacy curtains. Out of this Carroll makes a social comedy about respectability and propriety, based on Alice's adherence to her upper-middle-class manners and the disregard or incomprehension of this code of politesse by the Wonderland creatures, anarchists who won't be civil back and who ridicule her assumptions:

> 'Have some wine,' the March Hare said in an encouraging tone.
> Alice looked all round the table, but there was nothing on it but tea. 'I don't see any wine,' she remarked.
> 'There isn't any,' said the March Hare.
> 'Then it wasn't very civil of you to offer it,' said Alice angrily.

> 'It wasn't very civil of you to sit down without being invited,' said the March Hare.
>
> 'I didn't know it was *your* table,' said Alice; 'it's laid for a great many more than three.'
>
> 'Your hair wants cutting,' said the Hatter. He had been looking at Alice for some time with great curiosity, and this was his first speech.
>
> 'You should learn not to make personal remarks,' Alice said with some severity; 'it's very rude.'

Alice is the prim Victorian child lost in the madhouse, incongruously trying to maintain her sang-froid in the violent Duchess's kitchen or the Mad Hatter's tea-party. But she is also, like Carroll in life, someone who does not fit in: a lonely figure who goes through the books never quite connecting with anyone, sticking to her own path, stiff and virtuous as the Carroll Alice Liddell described walking upright as a poker.

> 'Only it is so *very* lonely here!' Alice said in a melancholy voice; and, at the thought of her loneliness, two large tears came rolling down her cheeks.

Beyond the social comedy lies the rich seam of Carroll's fears and doubts, animated by fantasy into archetypal characters and stories. The structure of the books – wild flights of fancy and adventure set within the discipline of a pack of cards in *Alice*, a game of chess in *Through the Looking-Glass* – reflects Carroll's own life, the neat donnish existence and impeccable manners enclosing the obsessive, imaginative loner who came alive and forgot his stutter only with little girls. Carroll's isolation and oddness are reflected in the tolerance he extends to the eccentric Wonderland creatures. 'One of my tutors,' wrote a Christ Church student in 1868, 'is the man who wrote *Alice in Wonderland*. He looks something like the Hatter, a little like the Cheshire Cat – most like the Gryphon.'[26]

At the other extreme are the characters Carroll knew he could never be. 'I pictured to myself the Queen of Hearts as a sort of embodiment of ungovernable passion – a blind and aimless Fury',[27] Carroll wrote, while the Knave of Hearts in his very name is the essence of the hot-blooded lover that Carroll was not, as well as a food-thief. Distrust of sensuality, of letting go, is a powerful undercurrent in *Alice*, and the other side of the idealisation of the prim, untouchable little girl. *Through the Looking-Glass* opens with a poem which hints at Carroll's horror of marriage and sexuality:

> Come, hearken then, ere voice of dread,
> With bitter tidings laden,
> Shall summon to unwelcome bed
> A melancholy maiden!

And both books are concerned with Alice growing up – in the cartoon-like images of her growing and shrinking in the first book, in the metaphor of her graduating from pawn to queen in the second. The chess game also plays out Carroll's distaste for passion, with the gentle, sad white pieces defeating the manic Red Queen. Like the Knave of Hearts, she is linked with food, voraciousness, unruly appetites:

> 'You look a little shy: let me introduce you to that leg of mutton,' said the Red Queen. 'Alice – Mutton: Mutton – Alice.' The leg of mutton got up in the dish and made a little bow to Alice. . . .
>
> 'May I give you a slice?' she said, taking up the knife and fork, and looking from one Queen to the other.
>
> 'Certainly not,' the Red Queen said, very decidedly: 'it isn't etiquette to cut any one you've been introduced to. Remove the joint!'
>
> 'What impertinence!' said the Pudding. 'I wonder how you'd like it if I were to cut a slice out of *you*, you creature!'
>
> It spoke in a thick, suety sort of voice, and Alice hadn't a word to say in reply; she could only sit and look at it and gasp.
>
> 'Make a remark,' said the Red Queen: 'it's ridiculous to leave all the conversation to the pudding!'

For Carroll, passion, lack of control, is associated with intellectual chaos and meaninglessness; much of his life, as an academic logician and as a self-contained bachelor, was

about keeping these twin evils at bay. But in the Alice books
they have free reign. The fat, sensual pudding terrorises the
polite little girl, flowers speak up to taunt her, she must play
croquet with unmanageable live animals as mallets. A special
terror of Carroll's nonsense universe is that the inanimate will
at any moment burst into life, so that Alice has no control over
the material world around her and loses her sense of identity
and direction:

> 'I ca'n't explain *myself*, I'm afraid, Sir,' said Alice,
> 'because I'm not myself, you see.'

> 'Would you tell me please, which way I ought to go from
> here?'
> 'That depends a good deal on where you want to get to,'
> said the Cat.
> 'I don't much care where –' said Alice.
> 'Then it doesn't matter which way you go,' said the Cat.
> '– so long as I get *somewhere*', Alice added as an
> explanation.
> 'Oh, you're sure to do that,' said the Cat, 'if you only
> walk long enough.'

It is hard not to see in Alice a comic, nonsense version
of a Victorian Everyman, bewildered by change, tormented by
religious doubt, terrified of an empty, godless cosmos.
Nothing, nonsense, death, extinction, lie below so many scenes
in both books. The puns and verbal jibes point to the
meaninglessness of language:

> 'I've had nothing yet,' Alice replied in an offended
> tone: 'so I ca'n't take more.'
> 'You mean you ca'n't take *less*,' said the Hatter: 'it's
> very easy to take *more* than nothing.'

The random violence – the executed gardeners, the
ink stand hurled at Bill the Lizard, the pack of cards tumbling
down on the little girl – builds up a picture of a mindless world
whose only certainty is death. It is there in the Queen's 'Off
with his head', in the fall of Humpty Dumpty, in the sudden
devouring of the trusting oysters:

'O Oysters,' said the Carpenter,
  'You've had a pleasant run!
Shall we be trotting home again?'
  But answer came there none –
And this was scarcely odd, because
  They'd eaten every one.

It is there in the Bread-and-butter-fly, a deliciously lyrical/comic image of change and death – and of a child's dawning sense of death:

'. . . you may observe a Bread-and-butter-fly. Its wings are thin slices of bread-and-butter, its body is a crust, and its head is a lump of sugar.'
'And what does *it* live on?'
'Weak tea with cream in it.'
A new difficulty came into Alice's head. 'Supposing it couldn't find any?' she suggested.
'Then it would die, of course.'
'But that must happen very often,' Alice remarked thoughtfully.
'It always happens,' said the Gnat.
After this, Alice was silent for a minute or two, pondering.

And it is there in Carroll's games of perception and shifting realities and madness:

'Well, it's no use *your* talking about waking him,' said Tweedledum, 'when you're only one of the things in his dream. You know very well you're not real.'
'I *am* real!' said Alice, and began to cry.

'But I don't want to go among mad people,' Alice remarked.
'Oh, you ca'n't help that,' said the Cat: 'we're all mad here. I'm mad. You're mad.'
'How do you know I'm mad?' said Alice.
'You must be,' said the Cat, 'or you wouldn't have come here.'

This dimension of Carroll's work has made him in our century a significant influence on surrealist and absurdist literature. 'Wonderlawn's lost us for ever. Alis, alas, she broke the glass! Liddell lokker through the leafery, ours is mistery of pain', writes Joyce in *Finnegan's Wake*. It goes to the heart of the books' expression both of the lost imagination of childhood and of adult pain at life's disappointments, intractabilities and terrors. In images of destruction, Carroll took revenge on a represssive society and on his own frustrations. In idealising a little girl, her virtue and innocence as she confronts a bewildering world, he poured out his own hopes and desires. By combining the two, he created a vision which is rich, extreme, eccentric; where mavericks are tolerated and life's oddness and despair are accepted. This is why the books are consoling; we quote them to cheer ourselves as we do nursery rhymes. His invented nonsense words – chortle, galumph – have become so familiar that they are included in the *Oxford English Dictionary*. After Shakespeare and the Bible, Carroll is the most quoted author in English.

Carroll finished the manuscript called 'Alice's Adventures Underground' in 1863. Among his child-friends at the time were the family of the children's writer George MacDonald – Carroll photographed MacDonald's daughter Irene with a seductively dishevelled hairdo and bare feet in a picture called *It won't come smooth* – and it was to MacDonald that Carroll sent the first draft of 'Alice' in 1863. MacDonald's six-year-old son, Greville, said 'there should be 60,000 volumes' of it, and Carroll was set on the road to publication. Charles Kingsley's *The Water Babies*, also a children's fantasy by an Oxford cleric, had just appeared, and 'Alice' was taken on by the same publisher, Macmillan. Carroll doubled the length of the original, changed the title – 'Alice's Adventures Underground' sounded 'too like a lesson book about mines' – and chose John Tenniel, who had made his name with drawings for *Aesop's Fables* and was also a *Punch* artist, as illustrator; Tenniel accepted because he liked the animals in the story.

Tenniel and Carroll, both brilliant, highly strung and difficult, proved a dazzling author-illustrator partnership: no one who has seen Tenniel's drawings can visualise Carroll's characters in any other way, and each artist enhanced the work

' "Talking of axes," said the Duchess, "chop off her head!" '
Tenniel based his illustration of the Duchess in 'Pig and Pepper' on
Quinten Massys' Flemish masterpiece, *The Ugly Duchess*.

and reputation of the other. Like Carroll's, Tenniel's art was at
once tough and formal, romantic, but dashed off with a light
stroke: he combined classical dignity with the breezy touch of
Punch, and brought to the *Alice* illustrations a sort of crazy
gravity – the Duchess in 'Pig and Pepper', for example, is based
on Quinten Massys' Flemish masterpiece *The Ugly Duchess* in
the National Gallery – which was perfect.

But he was Carroll's match in temperament too, and in
working together, the two men, each driven by his own
perfectionism, set one another on edge so maddeningly that
Alice was delayed, altered and argued over for years. 'Dodgson
is impossible. You will never put up with that conceited old
don for more than a week', Tenniel wrote to a later Carroll
illustrator, Harry Furniss. 'Don't give Alice so much crinoline'

and 'The White Knight must not have whiskers; he must not be made to look old', were the sort of instructions illustrator received from author. In return Tenniel wrote comments such as 'A wasp in a wig is altogether beyond the appliances of art . . . don't think me brutal, but I am bound to say that the wasp chapter doesn't interest me in the least'[28] – Carroll abandoned the chapter – and was painfully slow. Carroll, anxious that his child-friends were growing up, pushed for speedy publication, but when his mother died in 1864, Tenniel stopped work altogether, and when the book finally appeared in 1865, the crochety artist sabotaged it again, writing that he was 'entirely dissatisfied with the printing of the pictures'. Carroll recalled all copies and paid for a reprint; the second edition appeared for Christmas 1865. The tiny first edition of *Alice's Adventures in Wonderland* is now highly sought after.

The reviews, which were of the second edition, were mixed. The book was applauded as a 'glorious artistic treasure' and a 'triumph of nonsense', but *The Times* concentrated on the drawings rather than the text, *The Athenaeum* called it a 'stiff, over-wrought story' and the drawings 'square, and grim, and uncouth', and the *Illustrated Times* found the book 'too extravagantly absurd'. Only one reviewer, in *The Sunderland Herald*, saw what was revolutionary:

> This pretty and funny book ought to become a great favourite with children. It has this advantage, that it has no moral, and that it does not teach anything. It is, in fact, pure sugar throughout.

Following this luke-warm reception, the success of *Alice* was gradual rather than immediate, spreading by word of mouth from family to family. But by the time Carroll died in 1898, 160,000 copies had been sold. 'Few would have imagined', read the obituary of Carroll in *The Times*, 'that the quiet, reserved mathematician, a bachelor who all his life was remarkable for his shyness and dislike of publicity, possessed the qualities necessary to produce a work which has stood the test of more than 30 years, and still captivates young and old alike by its quaint and original genius.'

The importance of *Alice's Adventures in Wonderland* as a radical breakthrough in the history of children's literature can hardly be over-estimated. Today, many children find the Alice books frightening, confusing or just too difficult, but as the first and for a long time the only children's stories without a moral, they were favourites in the Victorian nursery. Bertrand Russell, who grew up in the 1870s, remembered the books as the best-loved among all his generation of children for this reason. Only Edward Lear's poems matched their freedom of thought and spirit. And as the first children's books to create an absorbing other-world of fantasy, the Alice books were enormously influential. Wonderland, with its own distinct landscape, language, logic, people; its precise physical characteristics, became the prototype for the escapist worlds of subsequent children's fantasy. Barrie's Neverland, Milne's Hundred Acre Wood, could not have been created had Wonderland not come first.

Soon after Carroll had completed the *Alice* manuscript, he was hit by disappointment. The boat trips with the Liddells were continuing, with the highlight a family outing in which Carroll was allowed to escort the girls home alone: 'Ina, Alice, Edith and I (*mirabile dictu*!) walked down to Abingdon road station, and so home by railway: a pleasant expedition, with a *very* pleasant conclusion.'[29] But two days later, when he asked to photograph the girls, something peculiar must have happened, for part of the diary entry recording his request to Mrs Liddell has been cut out, and a minor amendment made in another hand to make the entry seem complete, the numbered pages of the diary thus jumping from page 90 to page 92. It is almost certain that the missing page records a row with the Liddells, and that something improper to Victorian sensibilities occurred which led to this one page being removed.

No more contact with the Liddells is mentioned in the diaries for months, and at a Christ Church party later that year, Carroll records, 'Mrs Liddell and the children were there – but I held aloof from them as I have done all this term.'[30] A soirée at the deanery a week later is *'very* pleasant', and Carroll records, 'it is nearly six months (June 25th) since I have seen anything of them to speak of – I mark this day with a white stone'.[31] Next summer, however, he laments, 'During these last few days I have applied in vain for leave to take the children on the river i.e. Alice, Edith and Rhoda, but Mrs Liddell will not let *any* come in future – rather superfluous caution.'[32] Carroll may have been importunate in his advances, or Mrs Liddell may have felt the friendship had reached its social or emotional limits. She was a powerful, aristocratic and famously snobbish woman. The mocking jingle:

> I am the Dean, and this is Mrs Liddell.
> She plays the first, and I the second fiddle.
> She is the Broad; I am the High:
> And We are the University

buzzed round Oxford in the 1860s. She appears in Carroll's diaries as a dragon to be placated in order to reach his beloved, and somehow he must have crossed her irrevocably. He presented Alice with the manuscript copy of 'Alice's Adventures Underground', laboriously illustrated by himself with pictures of tense, gauche, bewildered-looking Wonderland creatures, and then with a unique copy of the published book bound in vellum in 1865. But when they met, Carroll aged thirty-three and Alice thirteen, she was 'changed a good deal, and hardly for the better – probably going through the usual awkward stage of transition'.[33] The friendship never recovered.

Carroll continued to be a shy, aloof and eccentric bachelor don. He poured much energy into making new child-friends; the actress Ellen Terry, whom he met as a teenager at this time, remembered, 'He was as fond of me as he could be of anyone over the age of ten.'[34] He kept up a myriad of interests, and used to bombard Lord Salisbury with strange proposals for the public good – a pamphlet on vivisection, a campaign to evacuate the natives of the island of Tristan da Cunha, where the whaling trade was failing, a scheme for firewatching stations on tall London buildings. He never got used to the publicity that the Alice books brought, and his behaviour in shunning fame was bizarre. His nephew recalled that once, 'when he was dining out at Oxford, and someone, who did not know that it was a forbidden subject, turned the conversation on *Alice in Wonderland*, he rose suddenly and fled from the house'.[35] He refused to acknowledge that the pseudonym Lewis Carroll was an open secret – to an American journalist visiting Oxford, he insisted, 'You are not speaking to Lewis Carroll.' Letters addressed to Lewis Carroll at Christ Church were returned unopened, and requests for photographs, even from family, were refused. ('I so much *hate* the idea of strangers being able to know me by sight.')[36] 'It is strange to me', he wrote, 'that people *will not* understand that, when an author uses a "nom-de-plume", his object is to *avoid* that personal publicity which they are always trying to thrust upon him.'[37]

He published academic works which were seriously received but which were shot through with the same sense of absurdity and rebellion as the Alice books: in *Symbolic Logic*, for example, he explains:

> A prudent man shuns hyenas;
> No banker is imprudent;
> No banker fails to shun hyenas.

Yet he was the most conventional and pious of men. A keen theatregoer, he made a point of walking out of any play which included cross-dressing. He maintained orthodox Church of England views, and was solemn about keeping the sabbath. 'Would you kindly do *no* sketches, or photos, for *me*, on a *Sunday*? It is, in *my* view (of *course* I don't condemn any one who differs from me) inconsistent with keeping the day holy',[38] he told an illustrator. Occasionally he preached sermons: 'I am glad to take the opportunities of saying "words for God", which one *hopes* may prove of some use to somebody. I always feel that a sermon is worth preaching, if it has given *some* help to even *one* soul in the puzzle of life.'[39] In puzzling out his own life, he remained logical, reasonable, and resigned. 'So you have been for 12 years, a married man,' he wrote to a friend, 'while I am still a lonely old bachelor! And mean to keep so, for the matter of that. College life is by no means unmixed misery, though married life has no doubt many charms to which I am a stranger.'[40]

Carroll was never tempted to marry, and was horrified when his name was linked with the Liddells' governess, Miss Prickett – 'Pricks' to the children – whose strict, humourless company he endured for the sake of seeing her charges. At thirty, however, when he first told the Alice story to the Liddell girls, he was a promising young don for whom marriage might have been a part of the future. By contrast, when *Through the Looking-Glass* was published in 1872, Carroll was forty, and he knew his life was fixed. The second Alice book has the same rich vein of nonsense but it is also sombre and wistful and it reflects an author who had come to terms with unhappiness. Carroll wrote it not in response to a demand from any child, but out of his own needs and longings. It is more lyrical and contemplative; it contains pure poetry like the almost elegiac 'Jabberwocky', and the voice of Carroll the quiet outsider, looking in on other more fulfilled lives, sounds throughout:

> 'I wish *I* could manage to be glad!' the Queen said. 'Only I never can remember the rule. You must be very happy, living in this wood, and being glad whenever you like!'

Alice's Adventures in Wonderland is a young man's fantasy and it trumpets the exuberantly bizarre. The Hatter, the Queen of Hearts, the Cheshire Cat, the mad Duchess are loud, boisterous figures who go out fighting. A decade on, *Though the Looking-Glass* is a mature work and many of its characters are gentler, more thoughtful, but terribly sad. At least two, subconsciously but surely, represent Carroll himself and his subdued, hopeless courtship of Alice Liddell, and these are the only two characters in either of the books who approach Alice with kindness rather than animosty or ridicule.

The first is the Gnat, who tries hard in his little voice to grab her attention and be her friend:

'I know you are a friend', the little voice went on: 'a dear friend, and an old friend. And you wo'n't hurt me, though I *am* an insect!'

He tells her jokes, tries to amuse her, but he cannot help talking of death, and Alice dismisses him into non-existence:

> But the Gnat only sighed deeply, while two large tears came rolling down its cheeks.
> 'You shouldn't make jokes,' Alice said, 'if it makes you so unhappy.'
> Then came another of those melancholy little sighs, and this time the poor Gnat really seemed to have sighed itself away. . . .

The second is the White Knight, the most eccentric mover on the chess board. He resembles Carroll in many respects. He has a 'gentle face and large mild eyes', he is a crazy inventor of games and gadgets ('It's my own invention'), he has a topsy-turvy view of the world and he believes in matters of the mind rather than the body:

> 'What does it matter where my body happens to be?' he said. 'My mind goes on working all the same. In fact, the more head-downwards I am, the more I keep inventing new things.'

He courts Alice with songs, begs for her sympathy, but at last points her on her way to be a queen (i.e. an adult), where, pathetically, he knows he cannot accompany her:

> 'You've only a few yards to go,' he said, 'down the hill and over that little brook, and then you'll be a Queen – But you'll stay and see me off first? . . . I sha'n't be long. You'll wait and wave your handkerchief when I get to that turn in the road? I think it'll encourage me, you see.'

He too is the failed suitor, but he has a special place in her heart: when he sings his song 'of all the strange things that Alice saw in her journey Through The Looking-Glass, this was

The White Knight: ' "I'm afraid you've not had much practice in riding," she ventured to say, as she was helping him up from his fifth tumble.' He resembled Carroll in many ways; Tenniel also drew him as a self-portrait, suggesting that he too found it easy to identify with the character.

the one that she always remembered most clearly'. It was the most Carroll could hope for himself.

Through the Looking-Glass was published, with popular success, in 1872. Alice Liddell was then twenty, and still Carroll's obsession lingered on; he tried to persuade Macmillan to bind a special presentation copy for her with an oval piece of looking-glass in the cover. In 1880 Alice married Reginald Hargreaves, an upper-class landowner whom she had met at Christ Church and who played cricket for Hampshire, and Carroll rarely saw her. There is a mention of her dropping by to see him on a visit to Oxford, and many years later he met her husband when he dined at Christ Church:

> It was not easy to link in one's mind the new face with the older memory – the stranger with the once-so-intimately known and loved 'Alice', whom I shall always remember

best as an entirely fascinating little seven-year-old maiden.[41]

'It is quite likely', wrote Carroll's nephew-biographer Stuart Collingwood, 'that Alice's marriage to Hargreaves may have seemed to him the greatest tragedy in his life.'[42] When Alice asked him to be godfather to her son, he refused.

He never found inspiration from a child like this again, but he continued to indulge his fantasies. In 1877 he notes in his diary a meeting with a girl 'who is about the most gloriously beautiful child (both face and figure) that I ever saw. One would like to do a hundred photographs of her.'[43] His later letters and diaries sound more sanguine, less defensive: in 1893 he admits to an artist friend who was drawing pictures and taking photographs of young girls for him:

> I was shy of writing plainly. *I* admire, very much, a back-view of a child *standing*, it's a lovely study of downward-rippling curves.[44]

He became bolder in his advances and was open in inviting girls to stay with him on his seaside holidays – he met them at Victoria Station or Eastbourne, and usually paid the fare – or in asking them for dinner. 'Would it be *de rigueur* that there should be a 3rd diner?' he asked one mother simply in 1892. 'Tête-à-tête is so *much* the nicest!'[45] Late in life, he took up what must have been his dream job of lecturing on logic at Oxford High School. 'The girls adored him', remembered a former pupil. 'He entertained them with written games on the blackboard. He was perfect with children, and there were always tribes of little girls attached to him.'[46]

Carroll's brother Wilfrid fell in love with a fourteen-year-old girl, also called Alice, waited six years and married her. But few of Carroll's other ten siblings married, and none did so before both their parents were dead; it seems that all were held in the thrall of a close family and found it hard to accept adulthood. At fifty-one, Carroll wrote that he felt no different from when he was twenty-one. He called the death of his father in 1868 'the greatest blow that has ever fallen on my life'. His sisters, recreating an adult version of their childhood idyll, bought and lived together in a large house in Guildford which also became something of a haven for Carroll.

He became less and less sociable as he grew older. 'The noise was too great for comfort. I weary more and more of dinner parties, and rejoice that people have almost ceased to invite me',[47] he writes in his diary; and later 'I decline *all* invitations', admitting that he was a 'selfish recluse'. He faced death with the lonely, brave rationalism that had governed his life:

> It is getting increasingly difficult now to remember *which* of one's friends remain alive, and *which* have gone 'into the land of the great departed, into the silent land'. Also, such news comes less and less as a shock, and more and more one realises that it is an experience that each of *us* has to face before long. That fact is getting *less* dreamlike to me now, and I sometimes think what a grand thing it will be to be able to say to oneself, 'Death is *over* now; there is not *that* experience to be faced again.'[48]

He continued to the end to write for children, but never produced anything as original or as broadly appealing as the Alice books. *The Hunting of the Snark*, a nonsense poem published in 1876, is forced and studied by comparison, though it contains magnificent characters such as the earnest, despairing Bellman whose job is endlessly to toll the bell. His last books for children, *Sylvie and Bruno* and *Sylvie and Bruno Concluded*, two volumes of a sentimental fairy tale with an evangelical message, show his fixations in no way diminished. 'It was in a London exhibition, where, in making my way through a crowd, I suddenly met, face to face, a child of quite unearthly beauty', says the narrator in the second book. Writing to the book's illustrator, Harry Furniss, Carroll pleaded for minimum dress. 'When children have . . . well-shaped calves to their legs, stockings seem a pity. . . . Also I *think* we might venture on making her *fairy*-dress transparent. Don't you think we might face Mrs Grundy to *that* extent?'[49] The dislike of boys is constant too: there is a loathsome child called Uggug, 'a hideous fat boy . . . with the expression of a prize-pig', who turns into a porcupine: a descendant of the male pig-baby in *Alice*.

This was published in 1893, and although the Alice books remained widely read, these last works were never popular. For by the 1890s, the tide had turned against Carroll's sensibility and the fashion was neither for little girls nor for sentimental morality. The last play that Carroll saw in London, just before he died, was J. M. Barrie's *The Little Minister*, and by the early years of the next century the English obsession with childhood had moved on to focus on little boys and particularly on

' "Who cares for you?" said Alice.
"You're nothing but a pack of cards!" '

Barrie's Peter Pan. Lewis Carroll died of pneumonia in 1898, aged sixty-five, at his sisters' home. 'How wonderfully young your brother looks', the doctor is supposed to have said to his sisters after his death. He marked, with his contemporary Edward Lear, the beginning of a tradition of English children's writers who were also particular psychological types: boys who could not grow up.

3

Edward Lear:
the Victorian Escape

I see life as basically tragic and futile and the
only thing that matters is making little jokes.

Edward Lear,
Diary

In the bitterly cold December of 1867, Janet Symonds, young daughter of the writer J. A. Symonds, fell ill in Cannes, the fashionable new resort where British travellers were beginning to spend the winter. Among the other English visitors to the town was an impoverished artist who had taken rooms overlooking the bay and was busy trying to sell his watercolours of the view. Just before Christmas, he composed a picture poem to cheer up the ill little girl. It was 'The Owl and the Pussy Cat', and the artist Edward Lear was soon to become famous as a Victorian nonsense poet.

Lear had already published some limericks, but 'The Owl and the Pussy Cat' was his first nonsense poem. It was written just two years after *Alice's Adventures in Wonderland* appeared, and Lear and Carroll had much in common. Each wrote his most famous work in the 1860s, each for a little girl to whom he was attached. Each was a lonely bachelor who loved making friends with new children – Lear sought them out in hotels across Italy and France by leaving poems and drawings at their places at the breakfast table. Each found adult social formality difficult and was more at ease with young people. There is no evidence that either read or knew of the work of the other, but both saw the absurdity in conventional Victorian behaviour, and created in response a nonsense world which held a particular appeal for children.

But, unlike Carroll and other great children's writers, Lear was not just a romantic escapee into the world of childhood. His empathy with children was so complete and wholehearted that all his life he felt like a child. He was too close to a child's-

eye view to idealise childhood as a separate state, and alone of
the fantasy writers from Carroll to Milne, he never sentimentalised children. Alice, Peter Pan, Christopher Robin, are
children's characters who are also seen from an adult perspective: they have a second, symbolical meaning for adults. But to
young and old readers alike, 'The Owl and the Pussy Cat' is
purely a poem of magical and happy escape.

Lear's strange fantastical poems chart his life like an
emotional barometer. The early limericks reflect his rage and
frustration when he first entered upper-class nineteenth-
century society. The poems of his middle years – 'Calico Pie',
'The Duck and the Kangaroo' – celebrate his escape from
Victorian constraint and narrowmindedness, but tell also of a
sense of alienation, his inability to fit in. The later poems, dark,
romantic and melancholy, like 'The Dong with a Luminous
Nose', are about the sort of lonely wanderer that Lear became
in his last years. His final work, published posthumously,
'Incidents in the Life of My Uncle Arly', condenses into a few
funny verses his odd, sad history.

Lear was a Victorian eccentric who tried to enact his
fantasies about escape and freedom in everyday life. Carroll the
Oxford don, Grahame the Secretary of the Bank of England,
Milne the sophisticated London playwright, all slipped part-
time into the world of childhood, but for Lear there was no gulf
between a public, adult, self and a private, child-like existence.
'Never was there a man who could so live into the feelings of a
child',[1] recalled a little girl he befriended in a Turin hotel in
1870. In his instinctive identification with children, he took to
an extreme the Victorian fixation on childhood.

Edward Lear was born in 1812 in Holloway, then a village
north of London. He was the twentieth of the twenty-one
children of Jeremiah Lear, a stockbroker who went bankrupt
when Lear was four, and, according to family legend, ended up
in the King's Bench Prison, where Lear's mother took him
caviar and sweetmeats daily. The Lear home, a smart Georgian
house on the corner of Holloway Road and Seven Sisters Road

called Bowman's Lodge, was meanwhile let to Orthodox Jews, who opened all the windows during thunderstorms 'for the easier entrance of the Messiah'. When the Lears returned, it was ruined.

During the smash-up of the family's fortunes, the children were separated. Like Carroll's, the Lear family was made up mostly of girls, and the younger children were allocated to the older sisters. Edward went with his eldest sister Ann, and when the family was reunited, his mother, worn out by childbearing, made it clear that she wanted no more to do with his upbringing. Ann, twenty-two years older, was a warm and supportive surrogate mother, but nothing could compensate for the sudden and inexplicable rejection by his own mother, and every word Lear wrote is haunted by a sense of desertion and nostalgia for better times.

His childhood was unhappy. He was a highly strung, thoughtful boy whose nervous temperament was complicated by epilepsy and short-sightedness. He was weighed down by the financial difficulties and arguments of his parents, unable to go out much because he was ill. There is also a hint that he was abused as a boy of ten by a brutal soldier-cousin, and that he came to see this as the origin of his own homosexuality. In his diary, he recalls this cousin who 'did me the greatest Evil done to me in life . . . which must last now to the end – spite of all reason and effort'.[2] Both his sexual preferences and his epilepsy – attacks were marked in his diary with a cross – were kept secret from even close friends.

Often shut away in what was known as the 'painting-room' of the house – in more prosperous years his father had collected paintings – Lear's childhood joy was to draw and compose comic verses. Like his adult writings, his early poems centre on eccentric people – 'Miss Maniac', who goes mad when her lover leaves her; a Chinaman with eyebrows two feet long – and are tinged with sadness. And from the age of seven, Lear suffered from the acute depressions – 'the Morbids' – that came to torture him as an adult. 'The earliest of all the morbidnesses I can recollect', he wrote, 'must have been somewhere about

1819 – when my Father took me to a field near Highgate, where was a rural performance of gymnastic clowns &c. – & a band. The music was good, – at least it attracted me: – & the sunset and twilight I remember as if yesterday. And I can recollect crying half the night after all the small gaiety broke up – & also suffering for days at the memory of the past scene.'[3] The juxtaposition of carnival energy and melancholy, the twilight scene, the snatching for happiness as it is pulled away: the memory calls to mind Lear's nonsense poems such as 'Calico Pie' and 'The Jumblies', where joy mingles with a sense of loss.

Deprived of the experience of growing up an ordinary, healthy knockabout boy in a loving family, Lear always longed for the perfect childhood that could never be his. As if to compensate, he remained in a sense always a child, unable to make the usual transition of growing up. He was in this respect typical of many great children's writers. Hans Christian Andersen, Kenneth Grahame, E. E. Nesbit, Frances Hodgson Burnett, the French writer Antoine de Saint-Exupéry, author of *The Little Prince*, Roald Dahl – all lost parents when they were very young and then never fully accepted adult responsibilities; all created in their work wish-fulfilment versions of the childhoods they had missed. Both Nesbit and Hodgson Burnett, for example, were three years old when their fathers died; both wrote children's books – Hodgson Burnett's *A Little Princess* in 1905, Nesbit's *The Railway Children* in 1906 – where lost fathers return in an unexpected and magical way. Each of these writers thrived as immature adults on a kinship with children, and created out of it imaginative works which generations of children have enjoyed.

Lear's way of refusing adult life was to reject everything that Victorian society held dear – responsibilities and the conventions of class, possessions and property, education and a profession – and to follow instead a wandering life as a landscape painter. He had little money, he never married, he had no home of his own until he was sixty. He identified most with children, who understood the niceties of conventional behaviour no better than he did. He made up nonsense rhymes for them, and he developed a baby-language of his own, with recurring misspelt words like 'stew-jew' (studio) and 'vorx of hart' (works of art), and joky signatures like 'Slushypipp', in which he corresponded with his adult friends. He called nonsense the breath of his nostrils; it expressed his view of the grown-up world as nonsensical, and affirmed his connection with youth.

Lewis Carroll always looked like a young man; Lear by contrast looked old early in life. He was tall, heavily built, wore well-made but unusually loose-fitting clothes and large round spectacles, and, as the portrait by his friend, the Pre-Raphaelite painter William Holman Hunt, shows, had already by his forties acquired the dense, bushy beard and warmly crinkled face that made him look like every child's ideal grandfather. He had soft, kind eyes, thick eyebrows and a big nose which he hated. An American girl who met him in Italy, remembered him.

> One day there appeared at luncheon sitting opposite to us a rosy, gray-bearded, bald-headed, gold-spectacled little old gentleman who captivated my attention. . . . Something seemed to bubble and sparkle in his talk and his eyes twinkled benignly behind the shining glasses. . . . I whispered to my mother that I should like to have that gentleman opposite for an uncle. . . . The delighted old gentleman, who was no other than Edward Lear, glowed, bubbled and twinkled more than ever. . . . He took me for walks in the chestnut forests; we kicked the chestnut burrs before us, 'yonghy bonghy bòs', as we called them; he sang to me 'The Owl and the Pussy Cat' to a funny little crooning tune of his own composition.[4]

There are stories about Lear in hotels rescuing children who could not manage a knife and fork from table d'hôte formality by drawing funny pictures and alphabets; on trains he would, as Carroll did, befriend children, take them on his knee and recite nonsense poems.

Children's affection answered some of the craving for love that was a legacy of Lear's early neglect. Often depressed, he became optimistic when surrounded by them. Quoting Sophocles in a letter to a one-day-old baby, he wrote 'My dear little tiny child. . . . I am sure you will not think me impertinent in translating what he says . . . because there has not been time hitherto to buy you a Greek Dictionary', and then congratulating her 'on coming into a world where if we look for it there is far more good & pleasure than we can use up – even in the longest life'.[5] Of the fantasy writers, Lear's relationship with children was the simplest and kindest. Children often remembered him as inspiring feelings of safety, security and well-being, and his friendships had none of the anguished, knowing intensity of Carroll's or Barrie's. He made child-friends and then let them go, as easily and carelessly as a child on holiday would, when he moved hotels or changed trains, and found new ones. His poems continue to appeal to children because his vision was essentially a child's vision.

His first role as an entertainer of children came in the 1830s. As a young man, he began a career as an ornithological draughtsman, and the first folios towards his book, *Illustrations of the Family of Psittacidae, or Parrots*, were published when he was nineteen. Soon afterwards, he was noticed drawing at London Zoo by Lord Stanley, on the lookout for an artist to paint the private menagerie kept by his father, the Earl of Derby, and was invited to live and work at their home at Knowsley Hall near Liverpool. It was Lear's introduction, at the age of twenty, to upper-class English society. When he arrived, he instantly made friends with the grandchilden and great-grandchildren of the house, invented rhymes and drew pictures for them, and became so popular that they left the grand, formal Knowsley dinners early to get back to him. The earl, a sociable and benign octagenarian, wanted to know why. 'Mister Lear, Mister Lear, come up here', he is reported to have yelled down to the artist 'below stairs', and Lear joined the earl's table and amused the lords and duchesses at his dinner parties.

'The uniform apathetic tone assumed by lofty society irks me *dreadfully*,' he wrote to a friend from Knowsley. 'Nothing I long for half so much as to giggle heartily and to hop on one leg down the great gallery – but I dare not.'[6] The contrast with his own family, sliding down the social scale into genteel poverty, was enormous; to him, much of the social whirl and languid conversation at Knowsley seemed ridiculous, and he felt overwhelmed and alienated. In the limericks he invented for the children, he expressed in fantasy the frustrations for which he had no other outlet. Employed to draw weird and wonderful animals at the famous menagerie, he composed even weirder and more wonderful verses. Into children's rhymes went his rage at snobby, constraining nineteenth-century society, his forlorn sense of not fitting in, his joky despair at what was absurd in life.

Composed for aristocrats by a penniless artist, Lear's limericks show the classlessness which was a feature of all his work. *Alice* was rooted in a don's Victorian Oxford, *Peter Pan* in the upper-middle-class nursery, *The Wind in the Willows* in the life of an Edwardian country gentleman. But Lear's poems, peopled by peculiar, fantastical creatures who have no possessions and who wander the earth, are, as Lear himself was, impossible to pin down to any class or place. Not until Roald Dahl's *Charlie and the Chocolate Factory* in 1964 was a classic of English children's literature classless in this way.

The recurrent story of the limericks is of an energetic and untameable individual who is destroyed by a narrowminded and vicious society, the omnipotent 'they':

There was an Old Man of Whitehaven,
Who danced a quadrille with a Raven;

73

> But they said – 'It's absurd, to encourage this bird!'
> So they smashed that Old Man of Whitehaven.

> There was an Old Man with a gong,
> Who bumped at it all the day long;
> But they called out 'O law! you're a horrid old bore!'
> So they smashed that Old Man with a gong.

> There was an Old Person of Buda,
> Whose conduct grew ruder and ruder;
> Till at last, with a hammer, they silenced his clamour,
> By smashing that Person of Buda.

The limerick's tight, double rhyme scheme complements the exuberant, bounding rhythm to suggest both the confining society and the rebellion against it. The accompanying pictures are frenetic, almost cartoon-like in their energy and exaggeration; Lear's early training as an ornithological artist helped here, and even in old age his drawings of people, round, beak-nosed and with arms fluttering like wings, still resembled birds rather than human beings.

Already in his twenties Lear was a typical clown: below the friendly, kindly manner, he was unhappy with himself and furious with the world. The comedy of people dancing, running up trees, marching up and down the Strand with pigs in each hand made his limericks popular at a time when most children's books were dry, moralising and unspirited. But Lear's limericks are also violent, anarchic and amoral – his revenge on society. Destruction and death lurk at the end of the most innocent lines; nihilism, the non-sense of nothingness, is the other side of their absurdist outlook:

> There was an Old Person of Cadiz,
> Who was always polite to all ladies;
> But in handing his daughter, he fell in the water,
> Which drowned that Old Person of Cadiz.

> There was an Old Person of Cromer
> Who stood on one leg to read Homer;
> When he found he grew stiff, he jumped over the cliff,
> Which concluded that Person of Cromer.

> There was an Old Man of Cape Horn,
> Who wished he had never been born;
> So he sat on a chair, till he died of despair,
> That dolorous Man of Cape Horn.

Chaos and incoherence is a keynote, with verses such as

> There was an Old Man of Corfu,
> Who never knew what he should do;
> So he rushed up and down, till the sun made him brown,
> That bewildered Old Man of Corfu.

predating Carroll's Red Queen, who has to keep running to stay in one place. Other distorted perspectives, too, anticipate images in the Alice books – both have puppies threatening to eat human beings, both have people falling into soup tureens, both have a claustrophobic quality:

> There was an Old Man on some rocks,
> Who shut his wife up in a box,
> When she said, 'Let me out,' he exclaimed 'Without doubt
> You will pass all your life in that box'.

And, like Carroll in Wonderland, Lear celebrates bizarre characters: people with peculiar eyes, poor chins, embarrassing habits, creaking shoes, most of all with the wrong sort of nose:

> There was an Old Man with a nose
> Who said 'If you choose to suppose,
> That my nose is too long, you are certainly wrong!'
> That remarkable Man with a nose.

Lear thought himself ugly and was obsessed with the size of his nose, which becomes in his poems the focus for everything about him that is different and odd. There is a man on whose nose 'most birds of the air could repose', another with a ring through his nose, and a lady whose nose reaches her toes; with such characters, he consoled himself comically for his sense of being apart. They reappear throughout his writing – people with noses like trumpets and like tassels and bells; the Dong with his large, complicated, luminous nose; the caricature in the 'Self-portrait of the Laureate of Nonsense':

> His mind is concrete and fastidious,
>   His nose is remarkably big;
> His visage is more or less hideous,
>   His beard it resembles a wig.

In psychoanalytic interpretation, the outsize noses are the unconscious phallic symbols of the sexually buttoned-up Victorian loner; whether one accepts this or not, it is clear that already in these early limericks Lear was drawing fantastical self-portraits.

He was also escaping into a world where oddballs are tolerated:

> There was an Old Person of Basing,
> Whose presence of mind was amazing;
> He purchased a steed, which he rode at full speed,
> And escaped from the people of Basing.

He recited this to the Knowsley children, and in 1837, the year Victoria came to the throne, Lear made his own escape from Knowsley and went to live abroad. He put his nonsense verses aside for almost a decade, then published them anonymously as *A Book of Nonsense*. It established itself as a favourite in the English nursery, but Lear was ahead of his time and received little critical attention, and when he planned an enlarged edition in 1861, taking in many new limericks and to appear under his own name, no publisher would accept it. Eventually Routledge agreed to distribute 1,000 finished copies if Lear arranged and paid for the book's production; then they changed their minds and bought the copyright for £125 – one of Lear's most foolish financial decisions, as the book went into many editions in his lifetime. In the early 1860s, however, reviews still dismissed it as merely old nursery rhymes. But by 1866, a year after *Alice's Adventures in Wonderland*, when children's literature was becoming more fashionable, Lear began to come into his own. 'Never was a book published that so exactly hit the child's mind as this one',[7] wrote a reviewer of the seventeenth edition of *A Book of Nonsense*. At this time, just as the climate of children's publishing was changing, Lear composed his first fantasy poem about his wandering life.

Lear was twenty-five when he left Knowsley and the nursery world of limericks and nonsense drawings behind. He never lived in England again, and instead pursued an exotic, rootless existence as a landscape painter in southern Europe.

In 1837, Lear joined a throng of early Victorian wanderers who were beginning to flock to the Mediterranean countries. For him, as for many of them, the official reason was health: he had been delicate from childhood, and his bronchial problems deteriorated in the north of England. His patron Lord Stanley offered to send him south, to recuperate, and also to learn to paint. Beyond lay the mixture of motives – dislike of claustrophobic England, hope of greater social and sexual freedom, the search for artistic and intellectual inspiration, the romance of sun-drenched lands, the excitement of the railway opening up foreign travel – which sent many Victorians into self-exile.

The eccentric artist-wanderer was a familiar Victorian type – William Holman Hunt, who painted scriptural subjects like *The Scapegoat* in Palestine, John Frederick Lewis, who recorded bazaars and harems in Cairo, were others. Lear, like many artists, went first to Rome, finding an enchanted city, bedecked with ribbons and bells, awash with aristocrats wintering in the sun and a pageant of clerics and cardinals in lilac and red converging on the Vatican for the festivities. Soon the *passeggiata* and the *trattoria* were part of daily life:

> At 8 I go to the Cafe, where all the artists breakfast, and have 2 cups of coffee and 2 toasted rolls – for 6½d and then – I either see sights – make calls – draw out of doors – or, if wet – have models indoors till 4. Then most of the artists walk on the Pincian Mount, (a beautiful garden overlooking all Rome, and from which such sunsets are seen!) – and at 5 we dine very capitally at a Trattoria or eating house. . . .[8]

In the next thirty years, Lear crossed Italy, Greece, Corfu, Albania, Palestine, Egypt, Lebanon, in search of the new and different, of spectacular views, unfamiliar scenes. In his paintings, he followed Turner in his response to the majestic in landscape, and conveyed it in vast canvases where man is either absent or a small figure dwarfed by the forces of nature. His pictures have at once a stern grandeur and a lush, romantic amplitude. Victorian taste was for tame, sentimentalised English landscapes, but Lear was drawn to stunning, foreign views – the close wood and mountain of the dramatically enclosed Santa Maria di Polsi in Calabria, for instance, or the forest pines between the great rock walls of Bavella in Corsica. The contrasting highs and lows of his landscapes – jagged cliffs, ravines, precipices; enormous, ancient trees; translucent skies and sunsets; the purple rocks and yellow foliage at Bavella – expressed something of his own romantic and manic temperament, and were to appear later in his poems.

To discover such views, Lear endured danger and discomfort. In Palestine his cave was surrounded by a hundred Arabs who attacked him and his camels in a demand for ransom money; in Corsica his driver beat his horses so violently that they careered off a cliff, killing themselves and destroying all Lear's paints and luggage; in Calabria, he travelled with a guide whose only words were 'Dogo, dighi, doghi, daghi, da', a refrain thought to have inspired the creation of the Yonghy Bonghy Bò. His reward was his freedom; he travelled mostly alone or with his Albanian manservant, and he painted and lived as he pleased. He had found his natural milieu of artistic exile.

Lear's paintings were never as popular as those of fashionable Victorian artists such as Millais, but by the 1840s his future as a landscape artist was bright. Working for the Earl of Derby at Knowsley, he had met 'half the fine people of the day', and these now began to be his patrons and friends. In 1846 his book *Illustrated Excursions in Italy* caught the attention of Queen Victoria, who invited him to give her drawing lessons – 'Oh where *did* you get all those beautiful things', Lear is reported to have cried when she gave him a tour of the treasures of Osborne House, her retreat on the Isle of Wight; 'I inherited them, Mr Lear', Her Majesty replied. Royal notice helped his reputation; the extensive network of British influence in southern Europe helped his work. On his travels, Lear stayed with an ambassador here, a lord there; aristocrats wintering in the sun passed through Rome and bought his pictures; others commissioned exotic landscapes and paid for Lear to visit unlikely places to paint them.

Around the same time, he began to be connected to English artistic society. He met Tennyson in 1849, and Emily Tennyson became one of his most sympathetic confidantes. Holman Hunt first saw some of Lear's sketches in 1852, and soon Lear had adopted him as a teacher/father figure – he always addressed Hunt as 'Daddy' and wrote to him in an intimate, nonsensical baby language. Wilkie Collins and the Pre-Raphaelite sculptor Thomas Woolner – Lear called him 'Uncle' – were other friends, and there are many records of Lear attending parties and artists' gatherings, as well as being a guest at aristocratic houses up and down England, in the mid-nineteenth century.

Yet he never felt quite at home, and all his life his instinct was to take flight from Victorian society. 'The moneytrying to get, smokydark London life – fuss – trouble & bustle is wholly odious',[9] he wrote on one of his returns to England. He hated the formality and competitiveness of society life; he had to conceal that his deepest longings were for men; he was poor and insecure and this made him shameless about asking for money and commissions from his rich friends. 'In a world where nothing succeeds like success, he has done himself much harm by his perpetual neediness', his patron the Earl of Derby once said. 'He has been out at elbows all his life, and so will remain to the last.'

'I feel woundily like a spectator, – all through my life – of what goes on amongst those I know: – very little an actor',[10] Lear wrote to Tennyson after Millais's stag party in 1855. A recurring problem was that close friendships made with rich young Englishmen abroad, in the tolerant expatriate climate of the south, foundered in snobby, restrictive English society. Lear's best friend was Chichester Fortescue, twenty-two when they met in Rome, later an influential MP, President of the

Board of Trade and Lord Privy Seal, and their warm friendship endured until Lear died. 'I threw the paper up into the air and jumped aloft myself – ending by taking a small fried whiting out of the plate before me and waving it round my foolish head triumphantly till the tail came off and the body and head flew bounce over to the other side of the table d'hote room', Lear wrote when he picked up *The Times* in Venice and read that Fortescue had been promoted. 'Then only did I perceive that I was not alone, but that a party was at breakfast in the recess. Happily for me they were not English . . . so we ended by all screaming with laughter.'[11] But when Fortescue married a rich heiress, Lady Waldegrave, this sort of cartoon-style behaviour was not always welcome; though Lady Waldegrave commissioned work from Lear, she treated him like a servant – visiting her lavish houses he was left to eat with the governess and given poky rooms facing the stables. Eventually he vowed never to visit again. 'Here . . . we are all humdrum middleclass coves & covesses, & no swells', he wrote back to Fortescue from the safety of Italy.

Another friend, Lord Westbury, outgrew Lear's nonsense when he became Lord Chancellor: 'Lear,' he said, 'I abominate the forcible introduction of ridiculous images calculated to distract the mind from what it is contemplating.'[12] Lear compensated by writing nonsense for Westbury's grand-children, Violet, Slingsby, Guy and Lionel, who inspired the heroes and heroine of his story 'The Four Little Children Who Went Round the World'. Others in public life thrived on Lear's nonsense. Evelyn Baring, an influential Consul-General in Egypt and Earl of Cromer, for example, was a dashing subaltern of twenty-two when he was introduced to Lear in Corfu, and the two formed an instant and lasting rapport based on baby talk ('deerbaringiphowndacuppelloffotografsthis-mawningwitchisendjoo')[13] and nonsense pictures; Lear also made a child-friend of Baring's son, and the twenty nonsense birds he drew for the boy were published posthumously.

Saddest of Lear's friendships was that with a gifted young classical scholar, Franklin Lushington, whom he met in Malta in 1849 and with whom he fell in love. The two had a romantic holiday in Greece which Lear remembered as the happiest weeks of his life: 'I do not know when I have enjoyed myself so much . . . we only complain that the days are too short. . . .',[14] he wrote to his sister Ann, describing the two men collecting flowers all day 'like children'. But when he visited Lushington at Park House, his home in Kent, the flower-plucking youth had turned into the stiff barrister and star Fellow of Trinity College, Cambridge, that he was in everyday life, and would barely talk to Lear; the Lushingtons, a strait-laced, gloomy, academic family, often spoke classical Greek at dinner or did not speak at all, and Lear felt rejected and despised. When Lushington was appointed a judge in Corfu in 1855, Lear followed him, but Lushington treated him coldly and advised friends against buying his pictures, and the affair was not rekindled. Lear, unable to paint or face his friends, sobbed in his room and wrote broken-hearted letters to Emily Tennyson: 'Say or think what one will, he is the most perfect character I have ever known – & I don't believe there are or will be any other half as good.'[15] After Lushington married, Lear grew resigned; he was godfather to Lushington's children and Lushington was his literary executor, although even here the conventional judge was destructive, disposing of most of Lear's papers and, among what remained, scoring out anything suggestive of homosexuality.

In the 1860s, when he was over fifty, Lear too thought of marriage. He turned his attention to a former child-friend, Gussie Bethell, the daughter of Lord Westbury, the Lord Chancellor. She was sweet-natured, unthreatening, devoted, but he was shy, terrified of rejection, and he knew his sexual preferences were for men. Six years after he first thought of marrying her, he plucked up the courage to speak, packed two trunkloads of clothes for a weekend visit to the Lord Chancellor's house, and asked Gussie's sister for advice. Emma Bethell was crushing and pessimistic, maybe because of the social gap between Lear and the Bethells, maybe because she sensed that Lear was not attracted to women, and she wanted to protect her sister from unhappiness and disappointment. After talking to her, Lear lost his nerve. 'Who *nose* what may occur? I am more cold & more cross than ever – it's so horridly dark and beastly. My only consolation is to buy toys for Charles Knight's and Holman Hunt's children',[16] he wrote after the failed visit. A month later he fled London and sailed for Cannes, and wrote his first nonsense lyric, 'The Owl and

'The Owl and the Pussy Cat went to sea
In a beautiful pea-green boat.'

the Pussy Cat', about two odd, sexless, cosy lovers who sail away for a year and a day and are married in their own quaint way. It was set on the vast, calm, sandy, moonlit seashore that Lear saw every night from his studio window:

> And hand in hand, on the edge of the sand,
>   They danced by the light of the moon,
>   The moon,
>   The moon,
>   They danced by the light of the moon.

and it was his first fantasy poem of hopeful escape.

Over the next three years, Lear settled in Cannes and then in San Remo on the Italian Riviera, where he had a villa built on the coast, his first home since childhood. It had spectacular views, a light, bright studio, and a garden full of olive trees and flowers. He could afford to live well there – the French and

Italian Rivieras, just beginning to be developed, were then still cheap and uncrowded. 'My ouss is phinnished. . . . I'm going to buy a Parrot, to walk on my terrace with, – so.' he wrote.[17] At almost sixty, he was more stable and tranquil in his expatriate haven than he had been for decades, and in these three years he wrote the nonsense lyrics that made his name. Unlike Carroll's contemporary nonsense universe, which is rooted in the Victorian England of trains and furniture dealers and Darwinian debate, Lear's nonsense emerged out of the Mediterranean landscape and is full of the joys of sailing away to exotic, calm, distant seascapes. Among children's writers, only Kenneth Grahame has a feeling for landscape close to Lear's. Both men preferred places to people. 'When I go to heaven', Lear said, '– if indeed I go – and am surrounded by thousands of polite angels, – I shall say courteously "please leave me alone! – you are doubtless all delightful, but I do not wish to become acquainted with you: – let me have a park and a beautiful view of sea and hill, mountain and river, valley and plain, with no end of tropical foliage. . . ." '[18]

This was what he invented in *Nonsense Songs*. The volume was published for Christmas 1870 and contained his happiest lyrics. Many of them were about mismatched couples – the Owl and the Pussy Cat, the Duck and the Kangaroo – with whom Lear, confused by his own conflict between homosexual longing and the pressure to marry, could identify. As in the limericks, Lear celebrates eccentric creatures who are trapped by social convention, but the mood is transformed and each poems tells the story of joyful escape and the triumph of exuberant spirits. The Owl and the Pussy Cat dance by the light of the moon, the Duck and the Kangaroo hop round the world, the Daddy Long-legs and the Fly play for ever on the beach, the birds in 'Calico Pie' fly away, the Nutcracker and the Sugar Tongs gallop out of the kitchen.

In 'The Duck and the Kangaroo', for example, one animal moans to the other:

> My life is a bore in this nasty pond,
> And I long to go out in the world beyond!

In response, they flee 'over the land, and over the sea':

> So away they went with a hop and a bound,
> And they hopped the whole world three times round;
>   And who so happy, – O who,
>   As the Duck and the Kangaroo?

In 'The Daddy Long-legs and the Fly', the insects dress up in their finery but their legs make them socially unacceptable:

> So Mr Daddy Long-legs
>   And Mr Floppy Fly
> Sat down in silence by the sea,
>   And gazed upon the sky,
> They said, 'This is a dreadful thing!
> The world has all gone wrong,
> Since one has legs too short by half,
>   The other much too long!
> One never more can go to court,
> Because his legs have grown too short;
> The other cannot sing a song,
> Because his legs have grown too long!'

Rejecting the world, they rush to the foamy sea and find a little pink and grey boat:

> And off they sailed among the waves,
>   Far, and far away.
> They sailed across the silent main,
> And reached the great Gromboolian plain;
> And there they play for evermore
> At battlecock and shuttledoor.

In the limericks, first composed in a formal English stately home, such mavericks are mostly destroyed by society. But in the nonsense songs, written in southern Europe, the eccentrics triumph by escaping to remote seashore paradises like the one Lear had found for himself. An undercurrent is his own nostalgia and the loneliness of abandonment – the Calico birds fly away to the refrain 'And they never came back to me!', the Nutcracker and the Sugar Tongs leave for a far-off seashore 'till far in the distance their forms disappearing/ They faded away. – And they never came back!'

1. Alice Liddell as a beggar girl, photographed by Lewis Carroll in 1859, when she was seven and he was twenty-seven. He wrote *Alice's Adventures in Wonderland* for her three years later.

2 and 3. (*left*) Lewis Carroll aged twenty-five, in a photograph taken in 1857 soon after he had become a mathematics don at Christ Church, Oxford. (*right*) Mary Hilton Badcock, photographed by Lewis Carroll *c.* 1860. This picture was used by John Tenniel as the model for his drawings of Alice in *Alice's Adventures in Wonderland*.

4. Lewis Carroll's family playing croquet in the garden of their home at Croft Rectory, near Darlington, Teesside, 1865. The family of seven sisters and four brothers was close and happy.

5 and 6. (*left*) Lewis Carroll in his sixties, at the end of his life. One of his last appointments was as lecturer in logic at Oxford High School, where 'there were always tribes of little girls attached to him'. (*right*) Edward Lear, painted by his friend William Holman Hunt in 1857. Aged forty-five, he already looked the part of the benign, indulgent grandfather-figure which his child-friends remembered. He thought himself hideous.

7. Bowman's Lodge in Holloway, then a village north of London, in a nineteenth-century engraving. Edward Lear was born here in 1812.

8 and 9. Two of Edward Lear's landscape paintings: (*left*) Pentedatilo in Calabria, where 'wild spires of stone shoot up into the air ... in the form ... of a gigantic hand against the sky' (1852), and (*below*) the Forest of Bavella in Corsica, 'an immense theatre confined between towering rock-walls, and filling up with its thousands of pines all the great hollow' (1870). The contrasting highs and lows of Lear's landscapes reflected his own manic temperament.

10. John Everett Millais, *Bubbles* (1886). Millais's portrait of his grandson became, through the Pears Soap advertisement, the most famous Victorian icon of childhood.

11. William Frith, *Many Happy Returns of the Day* (1856), an image of the happy and successful Victorian family.

12. The circle of Henry Charles Bryant, *The Lowther Arcade* (c. 1870). The Lowther Arcade was a popular Victorian walkway of toyshops running from the Strand to Adelaide Street. It was commemorated in a song of 1891, 'The Tin Gee-Gee, or the Lowther Arcade', the lament of a colonel on a tin horse priced at 1s 9d who spots another tin toy figure with neither sword nor horse offered for 2s 3d.

13. and 14. (*above*) Lawrence Alma-Tadema, *Earthly Paradise* (1891) and (*below*) Frederic, Lord Leighton, *Mother and Child* (*Cherries*) (1865). In a secular context, both paintings echo traditional Madonna and Child pictures.

15. Edward Coley Burne-Jones, *The Golden Stairs* (1880). For his celebration of female chastity, Burne-Jones painted the faces of women from among his upper-middle-class friends and family, but used the same professional model for all the bodies.

Nothing like these poems had ever been seen before. Lear's originality was to combine heady, earnest Victorian romanticism with the nursery-rhyme absurdity that was his own crazy nonsense vision. Only someone self-educated and outside mainstream literary life, living beyond the constricting expectations of Victorian England and writing outside its aesthetic conventions, would have had the boldness and freedom to do this. Sometimes he did it in a single phrase – the 'syllabub sea' in 'Calico Pie'. Sometimes the tones alernate through a poem, as in 'The Jumblies', on the one hand sublime and dramatic as his landscape paintings:

> And all night long in the moonlight pale,
> We sail away with a pea-green sail,
>   In the shade of the mountains brown!

and on the other comic and nonsensical:

> And they bought a Pig, and some green Jack-daws,
> And a lovely Monkey with lollipop paws,
> And forty bottles of Ring-Bo-Ree
> And no end of Stilton Cheese.

Where Carroll's nonsense is intellectual and logical, Lear's is poetic and emotional. Like his friend Tennyson's, Lear's settings are lush and wild; his tone is full of pathos and melancholy – the Fly's memory of his partner's song 'in former days gone by', the Duck following his 'own dear true/Love of a Kangaroo' to the ends of the earth. As a landscape painter, moreover, Lear's viewpoint was rooted in the physical world: his nonsense universe has its own precise locations – the great Gromboolian plain, the Hills of the Chankly Bore – and its own sense of place, of moonlight or sunlight playing on the sea and beach. Characters such as the Jumblies and the Duck and the Kangaroo seem to grow out of these landscapes: cosy, sexless lovers or friends, they are emblems of security and warmth in a fantastical setting. Carroll's world, harsh and threatening, offers a different, cerebral comfort; Lear's images and characters give instant consolation.

Lear appeals to the child, the dreamer and the joker, in all of us. When these poems were published in *Nonsense Songs* in 1870, followed by a second volume of limericks and illustrated alphabets, *More Nonsense*, in 1871, they were immediately popular, and Lear became famous as a nonsense writer. 'It is queer (and you would say so if you saw me)', he wrote home from San Remo 'that I am the man as is making some three or four thousand people laugh in England all at one time.'[19] Today, while children often find the Alice books difficult, 'The Owl and the Pussy Cat' is still a much loved children's poem and one of the few works of literature that children enjoy learning by heart. A century on, Lear's poems have not dated: simple and accessible, their overriding image of an eternal, beautiful, remote playground, the *leitmotif* of fantasy, is one that everyone can share.

In 1877, seven years after *Nonsense Songs*, Lear published *Laughable Lyrics*, his last book of nonsense poems. It included 'The Courtship of the Yonghy Bonghy Bò', 'The Dong with a Luminous Nose', 'The Pobble Who Has No Toes', and two poems, 'The Akond of Swat' and the lyrical 'The Cummerbund' – which first appeared in *The Bombay Times* – inspired by a trip Lear made to India at the invitation of the Viceroy, his friend Lord Northbrook.

Laughable Lyrics is very different in tone from *Nonsense Songs*, and reflects the fact that between the two volumes Lear had become an old man: living in exile, oppressed by memories, epilepsy, deteriorating eyesight. By the 1870s, his paintings were selling less well, and he knew now that he would end life alone. 'Every marriage of people I care about rather seems to leave one on the bleak shore alone',[20] he once told Fortescue. In 1872, his child-friend Gussie Bethell became engaged to a man, who, like Lear, was both much older than she was and in ill health; it seemed probable that had Lear had the confidence to ask first, she would have accepted him. He was jittery and bad-tempered in his disappointment – on his way to India soon after he heard the news, he boarded the boat at Genoa for Suez, grew furious about a delay, lost his temper, changed his mind about wanting to go, ordered all his baggage back to his hotel, relented, had everything returned to the ship, and finally sailed. Away from Europe, he looked back in his journal on the 'misery of some 55 or 56 years of past life ever before me – & ever I have to turn away from too much thought of it, by a decision that it was no fault of my making, but inevitable . . . always from my 6th or 7th year – year by year.'[21] He was almost certainly referring to his homosexuality, because after his death, his friend Lushington, whom he had loved, went through the diary and crossed much of this entry out in thick ink.

These were some of the thoughts which came to bear on the new volume. *Laughable Lyrics* returns to the poetic nonsense universe of *Nonsense Songs*: the same places and people are here – the great Gromboolian plain and the Chankly Bore and the Jumblies – but over them hangs a romantic gloom, and instead of the happy couples, many poems feature a solitary figure dwarfed by a harsh landscape or a vast seascape. Gone are the calm vistas of seashore idylls; here Lear described the awesome, dramatic views he had crossed countries to find as a young man, and which, as he recreated them in nonsense poetry, reflected his own emotional turbulence.

The opening of the first poem, 'The Dong with a Luminous Nose', builds up a terrific rhythmic momentum as an overture to the entrance of the sad, ridiculous Dong, and sets the tone for the volume:

> When awful darkness and silence reign
> Over the great Gromboolian plain,
>   Through the long, long wintry nights;–
> When the angry breakers roar
> As they beat on the rocky shore; –
>   When Storm-clouds brood on the towering heights
> Of the Hills of the Chankly Bore; –

The Dong is a solitary wanderer in nature looking for his lost love. 'Long years ago', he fell in love with one of the Jumblies; 'happily, happily passed those days', but when the Jumblies sailed away, the Dong was abandoned 'on the cruel shore'.

Now, like his creator, he is an eccentric with a too-large nose, both delightfully mad:

> But when the sun was low in the West,
>   The Dong arose and said; –
> – 'What little sense I once possessed
>   Has quite gone out of my head!' –

and desperately unhappy:

> You may hear the squeak of his plaintive pipe
> While ever he seeks, but seeks in vain
> To meet with his Jumbly Girl again;
> Lonely and wild – all night he goes, –
> The Dong with a luminous Nose!

He is Lear's most theatrical character, a Romantic in the tradition of Shelley or Byron, half menacing, half pathetic, and with just a shred of absurdity linking him to the world of nonsense:

> And all who watch at the midnight hour,
> From Hall or Terrace, or lofty Tower,
> Cry, as they trace the Meteor bright,
> Moving along through the dreary night, –
>   'This is the hour when forth he goes,
>   'The Dong with a luminous Nose!'

This poem and 'The Courtship of the Yonghy Bonghy Bò' are fantasies of failed courtship. The Yonghy Bonghy Bò also resembles Lear. He is poor and can offer little material comfort, but is lonely in his remote dwelling and wants to marry:

> Two old chairs, and half a candle –
> One old jug without a handle, –
>   These were all his worldly goods;
>   In the middle of the woods . . . .

> 'I am tired of living singly, –
> 'On this coast so wild and shingly, –
> 'I'm a-weary of my life:

But his aristocratic beloved, Lady Jingly Jones, is already

married in England, for the Yonghy Bonghy Bò has left it too
late to propose:

> 'Your proposal comes too late,
> 'Mr Yonghy Bonghy Bò!
> 'I would be your wife most gladly!'
> (Here she twirled her fingers madly,)
> 'But in England I've a mate!
> 'Yes! you've asked me far too late. . . .

The Yonghy-Bonghy-Bò.

He gives up hope and flees, the comic rhyme and rhythm
offsetting the pathetic love story in its wild landscape:

> Through the silent-roaring ocean
> Did the Turtle swiftly go;
> Holding fast upon his shell
> Rode the Yonghy-Bonghy-Bò,
> With a sad primeval motion
> Towards the sunset isles of Boshen
> Still the Turtle bore him well.
> Holding fast upon his shell,
> 'Lady Jingly Jones, farewell!'
> Sang the Yonghy-Bonghy-Bò,
> Sang the Yonghy-Bonghy-Bò.

In fantasy, Lear was working through his disappointments, at once indulging his grief and mocking himself. There are some happy poems. 'The Quangle Wangle's Hat' gathers all sorts of strange beasts – the Blue Baboon and the Orient Calf, and several creatures from other Lear poems, 'the Duck, and the Owl', 'the Pobble who has no toes' and 'the Dong with a luminous nose' – into a nonsense chorus in a moonlit setting much like that of Lear's San Remo garden:

> And at night by the light of the Mulbery moon
> They danced to the Flute of the Blue Baboon,
> On the broad green leaves of the Crumpetty Tree,
> And all were as happy as happy could be,
> With the Quangle Wangle Quee.

And 'The Akond of Swat' is comically boisterous and defiant; later, in a self-destructive mood, Lear told how the Akond of Swat, the Indian potentate-hero of his poem,

> would have left me all his ppproppprty, but he thought I was dead: so didn't. The mistake arose from someone officiously pointing out to him that King Lear died seven centuries ago, and that the poem referred to one of the Akond's predecessors[22]

But the notes of loss and melancholy in Lear's final volume are overriding. In the Indian poem, the heroine disappears when she is swallowed by an invented predator, the cummerbund. In the magical song 'The Pelican Chorus', the birds lament the loss of their daughter as she flies away, her voice fading as she goes to a 'lessening cry':

> She has gone to the great Gromboolian plain,
> And we probably never shall meet again!

And in 'The Pobble Who Has No Toes', the Pobble loses his toes by not protecting his nose – the hint is that he is thus emasculated, taken home injured to a female relative, Aunt Jobiska; Lear used to lament that as a boy he was cossetted by sisters and had not had a chance to follow typical masculine pursuits.

Yet though the tone is more intense than in *Nonsense Songs*, the child's vision never deserted Lear. These late poems are loved by children for their bizarre inventiveness, their cartoon-like images, the jokes and mocking rhymes and rhythms which are a counterpoint to Lear's lyricism, and which keep emotion and sentiment in check. The childlike word-pictures are irresistible – the Oblong Oysters popping up in the dark landscape of 'The Dong'; the daughter of the Pelicans married with 'a wreath of shrimps in her short white hair', and won by the King of the Cranes 'with a Crocodile's egg and a large fish-tart'. And details like the 'pea-green trowsers' of the King of the Cranes, 'the little Bheesties' twittering cry' in 'The Cummer-bund', are so simply charming that they could almost belong to the infantile world of Pooh Bear half a century later.

Laughable Lyrics was well received, although there was a general preference for the poems in *Nonsense Songs*, and the reviewer in *The Standard* criticised both the nonsense and the melancholy:

> We should not like to be condemned to read much of this kind of literature. Fortunately, in the present volume there is not much of it. The author must have supposed what he calls his lyrics to be laughable, since he gives them that title. If there is any man or woman whose features would curl, as novelists might express it, on reading them, we are certain it would not be with a smile.

Lear had another decade to live, and a few more poems to write. One was his 'Self-portrait', a typical mix of nonsense and pathos, which he composed with a friendly English family, the Bevans, living in San Remo:

> When he walks in his waterproof white,
>   The children run after him so!
> Calling out, 'He's come out in his night-
>   Gown, that crazy old Englishman, oh!'
>
> He weeps by the side of the ocean,
>   He weeps on the top of the hill;
> He purchases pancakes and lotion,
>   And chocolate shrimps from the mill.

Another was written when a huge hotel – for 'Germen, Gerwomen and Gerchildren' – was built on land between his villa and the sea, and his paradise home lost its views and its solitude. This is the background to the second part of 'Mr and Mrs Discobbolos', which shows his nonsense world at its most destructive, when 'Terrible Mr Discobbolos' blows up his home and family with dynamite:

> He lighted a match, and fired the train,
> And the mortified mountain echoed again
> To the sound of an awful fall!
> And all the Discobbolos family flew
> In thousands of bits to the sky so blue.

Lear sold up, borrowed money from friends and built himself another home: a particular trauma for one who, since his childhood eviction from Bowman's Lodge, had always distrusted property and possessions.

A second trauma, just after *Laughable Lyrics* was finished, was Lear's friendship with a young English neighbour in San Remo called Hubert Congreve, to whom he gave drawing lessons and with whom he fell in love. He dreamt that Hubert would become an artist, would come and live with him and learn to paint, be a sympathetic companion and soulmate. Lear had always been cheered by young people and now, in his sixties, he saw in Hubert the promise and hope that no longer existed for him. His feelings for Hubert grew more intense, there was a holiday together in Rome and Naples, and when, inevitably, the boy went off to study in England, Lear fell into the worst depression he had known. 'Tears blind me', he wrote. He recalled the unhappy time in Corfu when Lushington had rejected him, 'but then there was not the finality there is now: – then – there were unreal glimpses of light – : now – back returns the dark, "with *no more* hope of light". . . . I was never nearer to utter & total madness than now.'[23]

He rallied, visited Hubert in London in 1880 and took him to dinner at the Zoological Gardens, where he had met his first patron half a century earlier. 'You are just beginning the battle of life, and we will spend the evening where I began it', he said, and Hubert remembered that 'he was then absolutely natural and we were like youths together, despite the forty and more years that lay between us.'[24] Soon afterwards, Lear left England, and never returned.

Gussie Bethell, widowed, visited him twice in San Remo in the 1880s, and still the farce of his courtship continued. In 1887, aged seventy-four, he wrote in his diary 'more or less perplexed as to if I shall or shall not ask Gussie to marry me. Once or twice the crisis nearly came off, yet she went at 5 & nothing occurred beyond her decidedly showing me how much she cared for me. . . . This I think was the day of the death of all hope.'[25]

His last poem, 'Incidents in the Life of My Uncle Arly', was a fantastical nonsense autobiography, written in 1884 when he was in bed with pleurisy. It is a mock-ballad whose hero wanders away in youth over the hills to gaze at 'golden sunsets blazing'; he 'subsists' by teaching and selling 'Propter's Nicodemus Pills' – maybe an analogy for the views Lear tried to sell to tourists. He finds 'a First Class Railway Ticket', his invitation into upper-class Victorian society, 'but his shoes were far too tight'. He does not fit in, roams away, is homeless for forty-three years – Lear was without a settled home from 1827, when his father sold Bowman's Lodge, until 1870, when he built his first villa – and is either solitary or furious. The poem ends:

> So for three-and-forty winters,
> Till his shoes were worn to splinters,
>   All those hills he wander'd o'er, –
> Sometimes silent; – sometimes yelling; –
> Till he came to Borley-Melling,
> Near his old ancestral dwelling; –
>   (But his shoes were far too tight.)
>
> On a little heap of Barley
> Died my agèd Uncle Arly,
>   And they buried him one night; –
> Close beside the leafy thicket; –
> There, – his hat and Railway-Ticket; –

There, – his ever-faithful Cricket; –
(But his shoes were far too tight.)

Lear died in 1888, aged seventy-five, and is buried in the British Cemetery in San Remo. He told a servant to let his friends know that his last thoughts were for 'the Judge' (Lushington), Lord Northbrook, and Lord Carlingford (Fortescue): all had become pillars of the Victorian establishment while Lear, the anarchic artist, had turned his back on the world they represented. None of his friends came to the funeral. The wife of his doctor wrote, 'we went of course to the funeral. I have never forgotten it, it was all so sad, so lonely. After such a life as Mr Lear's had been, and the immense number of friends he had, there was not one of them able to be with him at the end.'[26]

'There was an Old Person of Philœ
Whose conduct was scroobious and wily;
He rushed up a Palm, when the weather was calm,
And observed all the ruins of Philœ.'

Inside the Secret Garden:

the Roots of Victorian Fantasy

'Ha!' said Dr Blimber, 'Shall we make a man
of him?'

'Do you hear, Paul?' added Mr Dombey,
Paul being silent.

'Shall we make a man of him?' repeated the
Doctor.

'I had rather be a child', replied Paul.

> Charles Dickens,
> *Dombey and Son*

In 1886, two years before Lear died, John Ruskin chose the nonsense poet as his favourite writer. 'I don't know of any author to whom I am half so grateful for my idle self as Edward Lear. I shall put him first of my hundred authors', he wrote in *Pall Mall Magazine*. A decade later, when Carroll died in 1898, the critic Walter Besant wrote that *Alice's Adventures in Wonderland* was 'a book of that extremely rare kind which will belong to all the generations to come until the language becomes obsolete'. In Lear's and Carroll's lifetime, English children's literature came of age. This chapter briefly sets their achievements in a literary context, and points to their influence on the Edwardian children's classics.

The golden age of Victorian and Edwardian children's books appeared to come from nowhere. Around 1800, the literary diet of the British child was skimpy. There were a few books of nursery rhymes, including *Tom Thumb's Pretty Song Book*, the earliest known book of nursery rhymes, dating from 1744, and *Mother Goose's Melody*. There were the popular chapbooks, later the Penny Dreadfuls, which pedlars sold for a penny and which recounted lurid stories of giant-killers and highwaymen, but these were comics rather than literature and were rarely approved by middle-class parents. Aesop's fables, which had a moral, were read, but there was little else that appealed to children. Fairy tales, to a modern parent the obvious literature for children, had been condemned since the Puritans as irrational, dangerously imaginative and immoral. 'Instruction when conveyed through the medium of some beautiful story or pleasant tale, more easily insinuates itself into the youthful mind than anything of a drier nature, yet the greatest care is necessary that the kind of instruction thus conveyed should be perfectly agreeable to the Christian dispensation', wrote Mrs Martha Sherwood, the high priestess of early nineteenth-century education, in *The Governess*. 'Fairy tales therefore are in general an improper medium of instruction because it would be absurd in such tales to introduce Christian principles as motives of action.'

European children did better, for fairy tales such as 'Cinderella' were celebrated in France in the versions Perrault had written for the French court in the 1690s, and in Germany in the new folk collections of the brothers Grimm. But in England religious and educational tracts, either dry, meek and unimaginative or fiercely moralising in their promise of hellfire and brimstone for the disobedient, were the prescribed reading for children. In Mrs Sherwood's tale *The Fairchild Family* (1818), Mr Fairchild shows his children rotting corpses to instruct them in the transience of earthly life. From Maria Edgeworth's *The Parent's Assistant* (1796), a mainstay of middle-class nurseries, a well-known story was 'The Purple Jar', in which a young girl is allowed by her merciless mother to buy a jar, which turns out not even to be the purple colour it was in the shop window, rather than a pair of shoes, and as a logical punishment can 'neither run, dance, jump nor walk'. 'Why should the mind be filled with fantastic visions, instead of useful knowledge? Why should so much valuable time be lost? Why should we vitiate their taste, and spoil their appetite, by suffering them to feed upon sweetmeats?' asks the Preface to *The Parent's Assistant*.

But the sermonising stories of Mrs Sherwood and Maria Edgeworth never caught the childish imagination, and already in the eighteenth century a definitive children's literary taste had asserted itself and hijacked three adult books for the nursery. John Bunyan's *Pilgrim's Progress* (1671), Daniel Defoe's *Robinson Crusoe* (1719) and Jonathan Swift's *Gulliver's Travels* (1726) were devoured and adored by generations of children before any specific literature was written for them. These three books, a mystical allegory, a desert island adventure story concerned with the nature of man, and a vituperative satire on humanity and society, were read not for their intellectual messages but for the elements of fable and romance on which each is based. All three create powerfully different other worlds, of desert islands and dream places like Vanity Fair or the Slough of Despond or Lilliput, of monsters and dwarves and giants, which have their roots in folk tale and myth. Their persistent popularity – adaptations of *Crusoe* and *Gulliver* are still children's favourites today – suggest childhood's instinctive affinity with the literature of fantasy, and children's desire to lose themselves in the other worlds of the imagination. Such fantasy worlds became the keynote of the children's books invented by the Victorians.

In the first half of the nineteenth century, a few unusual works ushered in the age of children's books. A humorous and fantastical poem called *The Butterfly's Ball and the Grasshopper's Feast* appeared in 1807, and its offer of pure escapist enjoyment was emphasised:

> Come take up your Hats, and away let us haste
> To the Butterfly's Ball, and the Grasshopper's Feast,
> The Trumpeter, Gadfly, has summon'd the Crew
> And the Revels are now only waiting for you.

The first collections of limericks, including *The History of Sixteen Wonderful Old Women*, was published in the 1820s; others followed in the next few decades, notably Lear's collection in the anonymous *A Book of Nonsense* in 1846. All these broke the mould of juvenile publishing in their levity and refusal to point a moral; all owed something to the English tradition of nursery rhymes. By the middle of the century James Halliwell's *Nursery Rhymes of England* (1842) had become a standard children's book. It was a scholarly and far-ranging volume and, along with its successor, *Popular Rhymes and Nursery Tales* in 1849, it gave nursery rhymes an enhanced status which fitted with the growing cultural emphasis on childhood.

The nonsense fantasies of Lear and Carroll owe much to the nursery rhyme, a particularly English phenomenon, and there is a clear link here. No other country has produced either nursery rhymes or nonsense literature of such quality or abundance. The nursery-rhyme scholar Iona Opie suggests that 'it's all part of being frightfully tough and not minding the weather . . . when you're feeling downhearted, you recite a nonsense rhyme to yourself',[1] and she sees the influence of nursery rhymes in many writers whom we perceive as quintessentially British, from Carroll and Dickens to Louis MacNeice and Benjamin Brittan. Carroll uses nursery-rhyme characters – Humpty Dumpty, the Knave of Hearts, the Lion and the Unicorn – and both Lear and Carroll's nonsense shares with nursery rhymes the weird, magical happenings ('the cow jumped over the moon') and the sudden, random violence ('cut off their tails with a carving knife'). Each took the very English mixture of fantasy and earthiness in nursery rhymes and built out of it a nonsense worldview shaped by Victorian England.

At the same time as nursery rhymes were acquiring literary respectability, fairy tales were beginning to be welcomed in English culture. In 1823 *German Popular Stories*, the first translation of the folk tales which the brothers Grimm had collected from oral tradition, was published; soon afterwards came the first translation of Hans Christian Andersen's tales, *Wonderful Stories for Children* (1846).

The Grimm stories, which the scholar brothers had collected from all over Germany, had the power of legend: their folk fairy tales had been told for centuries and are a unique art form. Their ability to entertain and enchant is unsurpassed; in so doing, as Bruno Bettelheim has shown, they answer basic cultural and psychological needs for even very young children by presenting in symbolic form our deepest dilemmas – sibling rivalry in *Cinderella*, terror of abandonment in *Hansel and Gretel*, sexual fear/desire in *Little Red Riding Hood*.

Hans Andersen was different: he invented the literary fairy tale, writing his own stories – 'The Little Mermaid', 'The Little Match Girl' – of a striking, near-archetypal resonance but overlaying them with a Christian, nineteenth-century morality and sentimentality which married well with the tastes of Victorian England. His tales became very popular in England; when he visited he was treated as a celebrity and invited to dine with aristocrats and ambassadors, and he became a friend and guest of Dickens. Like the later British fantasy writers, Andersen was a lonely, intense bachelor whose emotional links with childhood were so deep that his natural milieu was the children's story. His tales depend on a child's viewpoint, and he was never able to accept adulthood himself, resembling always Kai and Gerda, the characters in 'The Snow Queen', who are 'grown up but children still'.

Andersen and the Grimm brothers had an effect not only on English children's books but on all Victorian literature. 'In a utilitarian age, of all other times, it is a matter of great importance that Fairy Tales should be respected', wrote Dickens. Some of his books – *A Christmas Carol* (1843), *Hard Times* (1854) – are fables for adults with an anti-utilitarian moral. More broadly, however, the fairy tale shaped the Victorian novel so definitively that adult fiction became in a sense children's fiction – a natural development in a culture which made much of childhood. The invention of a literature for children was the apotheosis of a trend.

Victorian novels are moulded by fairy-tale themes and structures. They centre on children and their passage to adulthood. They are melodramatic, governed by preposterous coincidences and supernatural events, and have wish-fulfilling endings, usually the marriage of their young hero or heroine. They are mostly moral in tone, rewarding the good, punishing the bad. Their characters often have the give-away names of allegory – pragmatic and greedy Gradgrind and Bounderby in *Hard Times*, Bulstrode striding like a bull in *Middlemarch*, Murdstone a murderer with a heart of stone in *David Copperfield*.

Jane Eyre, for example, is a Victorian *Cinderella*, complete with ugly sisters, wicked stepmother and Prince Charming in disguise. *The Mill on the Floss* is *The Ugly Duckling*; Maggie the gawky child becomes a swan. In *Dombey and Son* Florence Dombey is Rapunzel, locked away to grow up alone, then released to marry her prince. Oliver Twist is every fairy-tale son who is denied his just inheritance and runs an obstacle course to prove himself worthy of his legacy. And even *Middlemarch*, which Virginia Woolf, looking back to the Victorians, called 'one of the few English novels written for grown-up people', has, in its story of Dorothea escaping the old ogre Casaubon to marry handsome young Ladislaw, echoes of *Rapunzel* with a dash of *Bluebeard*.

It was from this climate of adult literature that Victorian children's books emerged. Early Victorian children's authors rejected the narrow emphasis on education which had prevailed at the start of the nineteenth century and modelled their books on the newly popular fairy tales. Catherine Sinclair's *Holiday House* (1839) was a collection of stories about fairies and giants 'for noisy, frolicsome, mischievous children' whom the author feared were being driven to extinction by the do-goody evangelical tales of the moralisers. F. E. Paget's *The Hope of the Katzekopfs* (1844) was a cautionary fairy tale influenced by German writing. Ruskin's *The King of the Golden River* (1851) was, like Dickens's adult fables from the same period, a fairy story ending in an anti-materialistic moral, with allegorical characters reminiscent of the German tales – the saintly hero Gluck (happiness), the villain Schwartz (black).

As the genre matured, fairy tales developed in the 1850s and 60s into literary fantasies. These were sustained episodic stories set in enchanted places with strange landscapes, magic happenings and bizarre creatures, and they became the popular form of children's writing. This fantasy tradition included Carroll's Alice books (1865 and 1872), Thackeray's *The Rose and the Ring* (1853), Kingsley's *The Water Babies* (1863), MacDonald's *At the Back of the North Wind* (1863), Jean Ingelow's *Mopsa the Fairy* (1869), and Christina Rossetti's *Speaking Likenesses* (1874). Lear's nonsense poems were close relations.

In their imaginative energy and inventiveness, these books were landmarks in children's literature. They offered children's versions of the fantastical, escapist worlds – Wonderland, Kingsley's land beneath the riverbed, Mac-Donald's world at the back of the North Wind – which young readers had always enjoyed in the Vanity Fair of *Pilgrim's Progress* or the Lilliput of *Gulliver's Travels*. Although all the writers, apart from Lear and Carroll, retained a moral tone – figures such as Kingsley's Mrs Doasyouwouldbedoneby, Thackeray's Fairy Blackstick and Countess Gruffanuff give this away – none had the dull sermonising of the Mrs Sherwoods and Maria Edgeworths. All, by contrast, gave children's writing a serious literary quality – Kingsley, Thackeray, Ruskin, were all respected writers for adults – which it had never possessed before, and which marked the start of the high cultural status children's books have held ever since.

Of the Victorian fantasies, Carroll's and Lear's books were the most influential and lastingly popular. They had two broad effects on children's books. First, in establishing fantasy as a key element in children's writing, they determined the nature of all subsequent children's literature. Second, in discarding morality and teaching, and in making humour and satire essential ingredients, they set the tone of that literature in comedy and anarchy. Both these elements came to dominate in Edwardian children's books.

Before Carroll and Lear, children's books preached convention and duty, and criticised stupidity and bad manners. Since, children's writers have been on the side of the radicals. Edwardian writers shot their Arcadian visions through with irony as Carroll had done. Beatrix Potter's Peter Rabbit series opens with the image of the perfect garden, but:

> . . . .don't go into Mr McGregor's garden; your Father had an accident there; he was put in a pie by Mrs McGregor.

The rebellion and waywardness of the Wonderland creatures or of a destructive figure such as Lear's Mr Discobbolos can be traced in the irresponsible heroes of Edwardian children's stories – Peter Pan, Toad, Peter Rabbit – and on to contemporary subversive heroes like Allan Ahlberg's Burglar Bill. Another unworldly type, a sort of passive revolutionary, is the fond, foolish unknowing character, Carroll's White Knight, Lear's Yonghy Bonghy Bò, later Edwardian Mole, then Pooh in the 1920s, Paddington Bear in the 1950s and Roald Dahl's Big Friendly Giant in the 1980s. There is a shade of the Victorian ideal of innocence in all of them. None understands the norms of adult life; to children, and to anyone who feels at odds with his society, they are images of comfort, affection, reassurance. A belief in tolerance not judgement, individuality not standardisation, is a credo of fantasy, and one of its most liberating and consoling aspects:

> 'Tigger is all right *really*,' said Piglet lazily.
> 'Of course he is,' said Christopher Robin.
> 'Everybody is *really*', said Pooh. 'That's what *I* think,'
> said Pooh. 'But I don't suppose I'm right', he said.
> 'Of course you are,' said Christopher Robin.

The fantasy tradition held Edwardian children's writers in thrall. Barrie and Grahame embraced it in the Arcadian visions of *Peter Pan* (1904) and *The Wind in the Willows* (1908). Carroll's and Lear's crazy characters and talking beasts influenced Beatrix Potter's stories of animals in the Peter Rabbit series (begun 1902), Kipling's *Just So Stories* (1902) and his tales of fairies in *Puck of Pook's Hill* (1906). Even on children's books which were not primarily fantasies, the genre's emphasis on enchantment and wonder was a seminal influence. In the Bastable books (begun 1898), E. E. Nesbit introduced magic into stories about the ordinary lives of children – a magic carpet brings 199 Persian cats to a dining room in London, sand pits are filled with gold coins, children turn into giants. And in Frances Hodgson Burnett's *The Secret Garden* (1911), an early classic of psychological realism in

Rebellion and waywardness as portrayed
by Lear's eccentrics (1846), Toad (1908) and
Tigger (1928).

children's writing, the tale of two ill children and their recovery depends on an enchanted garden which recalls the one in Wonderland. Alice reaches the bright flowers and cool fountains of 'the loveliest garden you ever saw' with a golden key, and finds a new world. In *The Secret Garden*, a lost key opens the door into a walled garden of climbing roses, 'the sweetest, most mysterious place anyone could imagine', where a miserable, spiteful little girl becomes happy and a crippled boy learns to walk:

> They were the sounds of running, scuffling feet seeming to chase round and round under the trees. . . . It seemed actually like the laughter of young things, the uncontrollable laughter of children who were trying not to be heard, but who in a moment or so – as their excitement mounted – would burst forth. . . .
> 'Yes,' hurried on Colin, 'it was the garden that did it.'

The garden full of children, its resonance of the Eden of the soul, the enchanted place of the poetic imagination: Frances Hodgson Burnett distilled in the image of the secret garden a dream which haunted the second generation of children's fantasy writers, Barrie, Grahame and Milne, and, in the Neverland of *Peter Pan*, the river-bank Arcadia of *The Wind in the Willows* and Winnie-the-Pooh's cosy Hundred Acre Wood, inspired alternative realities as heady and intoxicating as Wonderland.

4

J. M. Barrie:
the Boy Who Would Not Grow Up

Nothing that happens after we are twelve matters very much.

J. M. Barrie,
Margaret Ogilvy

The Victorians liked little girls, the Edwardians worshipped little boys. Alice is virtuous, charitable and obsessed with good manners; Peter Pan is selfish, flippant and rude. The Victorian child is a symbol of innocence, the Edwardian child of hedonism. In fiction, the former is good, the latter has a good time.

Between Alice and Peter Pan, something like a revolution in the perception of children occurred. The idealisation of childhood remains in these years central to English culture, but a shift is marked around 1880, from an emphasis on the child as moral icon, emblem of purity, to a craze for the child as fun-loving playboy hero. The new image, in part a reaction to mid-Victorian social and moral repression and a death-obsessed court, was encouraged by the role of Edward, the Prince of Wales, as the irresponsible, pleasure-seeking playboy of Europe, and by the Edwardian decade the image had crystal-lised. Virile, outward-bound, ever-young men are the cult figures of the 1890s and 1900s, and a sense that life beyond youth was not worth living contributed to the fervour for youthful martyrdom that came in 1914. Leading up to it, the model of the dangerously attractive young man, immortal but in some way doomed, 'the lad who will never grow old', stands at the heart of thirty years of English culture: from Housman's Shropshire Lad and Wilde's Dorian Gray to Baden-Powell's new scout movement for 'boy-men'; from the portraits of Nineties dandies to the scandalously nude boys who filled the canvases of the modern British *plein air* painters such as Henry Scott Tuke. Of all these, the one who fixed most powerfully and popularly the sentimental, adventuring yet fearful Edwardian spirit was a figure from childen's literature, J. M. Barrie's Peter Pan, the boy who would not grow up.

If the Victorians set down the foundations for a cultural obsession with childhood, the Edwardians, with their attempt to turn life into a giant playground, brought it to its apogee. More children's writers from the 1900s are read today than adult authors, and from no other decade did so many lasting children's classics emerge: *Puck of Pook's Hill*, *The Railway Children*, *Five Children and It*, *A Little Princess*, along with *Peter Pan*, *The Wind in the Willows*, Beatrix Potter's stories and *The Secret Garden*. This was the period when adults applauded nightly as the boy Peter defeated the man Hook with the call 'I'm youth, I'm joy, I'm the little bird that has broken out of the egg'. Baden-Powell, founder of the boy scout movement, used to visit the theatre on consecutive nights to see Peter Pan because he found it so moving. The play in its original form packed houses every Christmas season from its opening in 1904 to 1915, when the famous lines 'to die will be an awfully big adventure' were omitted as insensitive on account of the war. It marked the end of the heady, playful escapism of the pre-war decade and of the glorious years of children's writing. Among the great children's fantasies, only Milne's satirical and nostalgic throwback in *Winnie-the-Pooh* was still to come.

Peter Pan played an important role in the adulation of youth and its denouement. Its creator, James Barrie, born in 1860, was a mid-Victorian who grew up when the cult of childhood already held full sway. His personal tragedy, as well as his public success, was that the idea of boyhood always held his imagination fast, and that he was in life the archetypal hero of *fin de siècle* fiction: the eternal boy. Both *Peter Pan* and *The Wind in the Willows*, the fantasy by Barrie's contemporary Kenneth Grahame, are the products of individual psychologies and temperaments which happened to coincide with the child-obsessed spirit of the age.

What makes Barrie unique among the fantasy writers is the

chilling interaction between his art and his life. For other children's writers, fantasy remained an escapist paradise never put to the test. But in an uncanny way Barrie's fantasy – of remaining always a boy, of inheriting a group of lost boys – came true after he had written it and then turned, in life, to tragedy and disillusion. In the creation of his dream of eternal youth and in its cruel unmasking, Barrie is a cornerstone in both the story of children's literature and in the history of English culture in the first decades of this century.

Peter Pan is the dream figure of an age which declined to grow up. He is a character unlike any other in fiction, yet he is also the most famous of a cluster of Pans, and of a stampede of eager, ever-young men, who appeared in English art and literature in the late nineteenth and early twentieth centuries. It is both as a symbol of this age, and as an expression of the longings and fears in Barrie's psyche, that the power and terror of this icon of childhood is best revealed.

Pan, the Greek God of nature who was half-boy, half-beast, is a figure who recurs through European culture, especially after the Romantics. But he became a natural and pervasive Edwardian god: a playful, wild outdoor hero who never ages, combining in one image the delights of rural and childhood retreat. Kenneth Grahame wrote essays in his praise – 'The Lost Centaur', 'The Rural Pan' – and Pan is the spiritual hero of *The Wind in the Willows*, the 'Piper at the Gates of Dawn' who is lord of a community of boy-animals rather as Peter Pan presides over the Lost Boys. Elsewhere, extraordinary versions of Pan abound around this time. 'Pan is not dead', wrote Robert Louis Stevenson in an influential essay, 'Pan's Pipes', in *Virginibus Puerisque* (1881), 'but of all the classic hierarchy alone survives in triumph – his joyful measures . . . to which the whole earth treads in choral harmony. To this music the young lambs bound as to a tabor, and the London shop-girl skips rudely in the dance.' Maurice Hewlett's play *Pan and the Young Shepherds* opened in 1898 with the line 'Boy, boy, wilt thou be a boy for ever?' In a cruel short story, Saki has a woman punished by death for doubting the existence of Pan. Kipling's *Puck of Pook's Hill* (1906) stars Pan, Aubrey Beardsley's novel *Under the Hill* (1904) is about an orgy of satyrs and shepherdesses, and the children's classic *The Secret Garden* has a Pan-like figure, Dickon, a rural wanderer with supernatural powers. Burne-Jones drew a whimsical Pan; C. H. Shannon published woodcuts of Pan in *The Dial*. Charles Sims's picture *The Little Faun* (1908) has a mischievous centaur disrupt a dinner party, and his *The Beautiful is Fled*, with a tiny faun shivering in a bare winter river landscape, suggests the unearthly wistfulness of the apparition of Pan in *The Wind in the Willows*.

Peter Pan, whose horned cap, rural attire – he is 'clad in skeleton leaves and the juices that ooze from trees' – and pan pipes are the only remnants of his descent from the Greek centaur, is the most eccentric and the most human of all these creatures. He could not have come about without the cultural obsession with Pan, but he belongs as much to the popular archetype of the immortal young man which was developing in the 1880s when Barrie was forming literary ambitions.

Barrie was five when *Alice* appeared in 1865, and by the time he began to write, the famous icons of childhood tended to be boys rather than girls. Millais's portrait of his grandson in *Bubbles*, reproduced in homes across the country in the Pears Soap advertisement, and Little Lord Fauntleroy, the best-selling do-gooder in the velvet suit and Vandyke collar, were the crazes of the 1880s, and *Treasure Island*, *Kidnapped* and *Huckleberry Finn* were all giving the boys' adventure story new success. Barrie, who believed that 'nothing that happens after we are twelve matters very much', was in his element.

In 1888, George Moore, who had lived in Paris, heralded the craze for the young man with *Confessions of a Young Man*. Moore lamented that while the nineteenth century in France had been the age of the young man, in England the century had belonged to the girl, and must now be won for the youth. But the change was already under way. Moore was writing four years after Huysmans' novel *A Rebours*, which has a dandy

Famous Edwardian versions of Pan: Barrie's Peter Pan, in Mabel
Lucie Attwell's illustration for *Peter Pan and Wendy* (1911), and
Kenneth Grahame's Piper at the Gates of Dawn, in E. H.
Shephard's illustration.

debauchee hero, Des Esseintes, drooling over books and ornaments and perfumes and sexual exploits, had caused a sensation in Paris. By the end of the 1880s, the novel was a bible of decadence for the London fast set, and the dandy, with his cult of male beauty and hint of psychological perversity, became a fashionable English type.

The British writers closest to Paris, Walter Pater and Oscar Wilde, brought the dandy home, and it was Wilde, the flamboyant wit who wore dyed green carnations as a symbol of youth and went into mourning on his birthdays because they brought old age closer, who most embodied the character of the continental aesthete poseur. In the 1880s, both Wilde and Pater wrote works which focus on the beautiful young man, and both prophetically identify him with sacrifice, death, martyrdom to youth.

Wilde's fairy tales, collected in *The Happy Prince* (1888), are not stories for children at all but fables on the subject closest to his heart: the sacrificial nature of love between men in a brash and heartless society. In the story 'The Selfish Giant', a dying giant is taught to enjoy a glorious garden by falling in love with a small boy whom he loved 'the best because he had kissed him'. 'The Happy Prince' is a love story between a golden statue of a young prince overlooking a sordid, prejudiced town, and a lithe male swallow who brings him love and dies for him. In metaphor, Wilde trembles on the brink: 'But you must kiss me on the lips, for I love you', says the prince to the bird.

Wilde's characters die for love in a hostile world: a horribly accurate vision of his own downfall and death twelve years later. Pater's novel *Marius the Epicurean* (1885) recommends withdrawal from society into a world of aestheticism. Flavian, the dandy-poet hero, is an idealised youth who 'as with the privileges of a natural aristocracy, believed only in himself, in the brilliant and mainly sensuous gifts he had, or meant to acquire'. He dies young, his promise unfulfilled and unfulfillable, the first of a series of self-indulgent heroes who choose youthful immortality rather than ageing. In fairyland over a decade later, Peter Pan makes the same choice:

'Would you send me to school?' he inquired craftily.
'Yes.'
'And then to an office?'
'I suppose so.'
'Soon I should be a man?'
'Very soon.'
'I don't want to go to school and learn solemn things,'
he told her passionately. . . . 'Keep back, lady, no one is
going to catch me and make me a man.'

A quarter of a century after Pater, Max Beerbohm's
hero the Duke of Dorset in *Zuleika Dobson* (1911) drowns
himself in the Cherwell to preserve for ever his image as a
brilliant young undergraduate. His tragic type became so
familiar that W. S. Gilbert mocked it in his 'greenery yallery
foot-in-the-grave young man'.

Dandy of the decade was Dorian Gray, who in Wilde's 1891
novella swaps his mortality with his portrait, so remaining
young while the portrait ages. He ushered in the *fin de siècle*
model of narcissism. John Singer Sargent's 1894 portrait of the
effeminately posed artist Graham Robertson, a friend of
Kenneth Grahame's, in a sweeping overcoat, cane in hand,
chow curled up at his feet, expression perplexed, has come to
typify this character. 'Mr Sargent has realized once and for ever
the type of fashionable young man of artistic tendencies of this
end of the century', approved George Moore.[1] Sickert's 1895
portrait of the dying Aubrey Beardsley, 'the loose-limbed, lank
figure so immaculately dressed in black cut away coat and silk
hat, who carried his lemon yellow kid gloves in his long white
hands, his lean wrists showing naked beyond his cuffs',[2] is
another example. In fiction, Sherlock Holmes and Raffles are
classic dandies. By the end even Queen Victoria had her court
dandy, Alick Yorke, a performing theatrical who wore flowers
in his buttonhole, jewelled rings and flashy suits, and wafted in
and out in a cloud of scent.

Peter Pan, the narcissist who has absolutely no memory and
so can live only for the moment, has a whiff of the pleasure-
principle that the French found so attractive, and the English

so decadent, in Pater and Wilde. Pater in *The Renaissance* (1873) courted scandal by advising young men 'to burn always with this hard, gem-like flame, to maintain this ecstasy', to seek 'the highest quality to your moments as they pass, and simply for those moments' sake'; Peter Pan experiences 'ecstasies innumerable that other children can never know'. But he encapsulates too the boyishness which was the Nineties English counterpart to the sophisticated French youth. He is an asexual child, not a young man; he belongs with the boyish heroes of Beardsley, Rhodes, Henley, H. G. Wells's Kipps and Mr Polly, Kipling's Kim, later P. G. Wodehouse's naif Bertie Wooster. Even Pater in *Marius* cannot resist the Victorian public school spirit; for his young Spartans, there are 'no warm baths allowed; a daily plunge in their river required. . . . Youthful beauty and strength in perfect service – a manifestation of the true and genuine Hellenism, though it may make one think of the novices at school in some Gothic cloister, of our own English school.'

In an English context, the ideal of youth is not Wildean aestheticism but asceticism: duty, team spirit, male fellowship, the outdoor life, sacrifice not to art and grace but to patriotism. The young man as naif, helplessly unaware, beautiful, and doomed, is the type Housman fixed in *A Shropshire Lad* (1896), with poems such as 'To an Athlete Dying Young', with admonitions to 'stand and fight and see your slain/And take the bullet in your brain', and in its cast of 'luckless lads' snatched from the lush English countryside to be wartime martyrs. Housman's lyrical evocation of 'the lads that will die in their glory and never be old' is suffused with patriotism and nostalgia for boyish innocence:

> Into my heart an air that kills
>   From yon far country blows:
> What are those blue remembered hills,
>   What spires, what farms are those?
>
> That is the land of lost content,
>   I see it shining plain,

> The happy highways where I went
> And cannot come again.

'To my generation no other English poet seemed so perfectly to express the sensibility of the male adolescent', wrote W. H. Auden.[3] There are echoes throughout contemporary popular literature and art. Marie Corelli's hero in *Boy* (1900) sobs 'I did want to be a real English boy! – a real, real English boy' before signing up for the Transvaal and dying. In Charles Spencelayh's *Dreams of Glory* (1900) a sleeping boy dreams of Boer War romance in a gush of sentimental heroism. *Peter Pan*, where Wendy as the emblem of British mothers gives up her brood to patriotic death on the gangplank, emerged from this climate.

The same spirit, with the undercurrent of homosexuality that is inescapable from Pater and Wilde to Housman and Brooke, informs the Kipling of *Barrack Room Ballads*, wallowing in war and stench and male bonding 'when two young men stand face to face', and the imperial boy-man idealism of Baden-Powell, who used to get a frisson on watching soldiers 'trooping in to be washed in nature's garb, with their strong well-built naked wonderfully male bodies'[4] (women by comparison are 'pinkish, whitish, dollish') and went to Charterhouse to watch naked boys being photographed in the grounds. It guaranteed a market for risqué pictures like Simeon Solomon's *Love Among the Schoolboys*, believed to have once been owned by Oscar Wilde. And it inspired Rupert Brooke, the perfect public schoolboy for whom boyhood, as for Barrie, represented an Eden impossible to recapture: 'I have been happier at Rugby than I can find words to say. As I look back at five years there, I seem to see almost every hour as golden and radiant and always increasing in beauty . . . and I could not, and cannot, hope for or even imagine such happiness elsewhere.'[5] Where else to go but death, as Brooke rapturised in 1914:

> Now, God be thanked Who has matched us with His hour,
> And caught our youth, and wakened us from sleeping,

With hand made sure, clear eye, and sharpened power,
To turn, as swimmers into cleanness leaping.

Brooke's famous sonnet published on the outbreak of
hostilities fixes the sentiment that the war came as a climax to
the values of 'youthful beauty and strength in perfect service'
which had obsessed a generation since Pater. It was an answer
to all the boys who could not face growing up, a relief for the
youths who could see no other way forward from the heady
days of plunging into rivers and basking afterwards in
seemingly endless sunlight. Many writers had contributed to
this mood; Barrie stood at the heart of it.

Reviewing the novel *A Window in Thrums* in *The Scotsman*, a
critic once called Barrie 'a man who would make copy out of his
grandmother's bones'. No doubt he saw his chance with the
theme of childhood, which runs through every line he wrote,
but it was a personal obsession with boyhood which shaped his
work.

In his early years, Jamie Barrie grew up in a large, happy
family in Kirriemuir in northern Scotland, where his father
was a weaver with a reasonable income and his mother
encouraged educational ambition in all her children. But when
Jamie was six, the most gifted of them, his brother David, died
at thirteen in a skating accident, and his mother, in shock and
grief, retired alone to her darkened bedroom for months,
leaving the rest of the family to cope as best as they could.
Barrie, sobbing on the stairs at his abandonment, was one day
sent by an older sister to try to console her; he later recalled:

> Then the voice said more anxiously 'Is that you?' again. I
> thought it was the dead boy she was speaking to, and I said
> in a little lonely voice, 'No, it's no' him, it's just me'. Then
> I heard a cry, and my mother turned in bed, and though it
> was dark I knew that she was holding out her arms.[6]

Thus began Barrie's childhood mission to comfort his
mother by becoming so like David that she should not see the
difference. He dressed in his brother's clothes, learned his

brother's way of whistling, and became fixated on the idea of remaining always a boy. Although twenty years later his mother still fell asleep speaking to the dead boy, she and James grew passionately close – he wrote to her every day, and she slept with his latest letter under her pillow, until she died when he was thirty-five. In a sense he became the living version of the son who by dying had remained ever young. 'When I became a man, he was still a boy of thirteen', wrote Barrie.[7] But he, too, in a different way, failed to grow up.

To please his mother, he matriculated at Edinburgh University, but at eighteen he was uneasy in the company of men and his notebooks from this time are full of a terror of adulthood: 'Greatest horror – dream I am married – wake up shrieking. . . . Grow up and have to give up marbles – awful thought.'

He felt especially threatened by fast undergraduate talk about women – 'far finer and nobler things in the world than loving a girl and getting her' – and showed little interest here himself. And he continued to look like a pre-pubescent boy: short since childhood, he grew to just over five feet tall, with a thin, youthful figure, a reedy, high-pitched voice and a painfully shy and nervous manner. 'Six feet three inches', he wrote when he was sixty. 'If I had really grown to this it would have made a great difference in my life. I would not have bothered turning out reels of printed matter. . . . The things I could have said to [ladies] if my legs had been longer.'[8]

In the early 1880s, stoked up on maternal ambition and dreams of literary glory, Barrie went south to England with a burning desire to forge a name as journalist and novelist. 'There are few more impressive sights in the world than a Scotsman on the make,' he later wrote.[9] He besieged editors with a flurry of offerings, but those most enthusiastically taken up were on an inevitable subject – his mother. Still too close to his own childhood to turn it to copy, he based a crowd of articles and then four books on the stories his mother had told him about her girlhood in Kirriemuir. The first book, *Auld Licht Idylls* (1888), brought acclaim; the sequels, *A Window in*

Thrums and *The Little Minister* – hailed on a front page review in the *National Observer* as 'a Book of Genius' – make Barrie a household name.

Barrie was writing when romantic accounts of childhood for adults were becoming a fashionable new genre. Robert Louis Stevenson's *Virginibus Puerisque*, with essays such as 'Child's Play', set the trend; Kenneth Grahame's idealisation of his childhood, *The Golden Age* and *Dream Days*, were Nineties bestsellers. Sentimental, whimsical, yet with a hard nose for commercial success, Barrie fitted his preoccupations to the times. He followed up his novels with some light-weight plays which were also well-received. He got a fan letter from his hero Stevenson, he became friends with influential editors like W. E. Henley, who ran the *National Observer*, and by his early thirties he was already a big splash in the London literary pool.

But he was also the little man who wrote home every day and could still barely talk to a girl without twisting his tongue into knots. He always described himself as a 'man's man', and his happiest pleasures continued to be boyish – founding a cricket club in 1890, the Allahakbars (Arabic for 'Heaven help us', later changed to the Allahakbarries), in which literary friends such as Conan Doyle and P. G. Wodehouse played, for example. Beyond this, there were crushes on actresses who ignored him, fears that he was capable only of the sentimentality in his books and not of love, anxious third-person musings ('perhaps the curse of his life was that he never "had a woman" ') in the notebooks he carried everywhere.

But in 1892, when he was thirty-two, his play *Walker, London* opened with the actress Mary Ansell in a leading role. She was young, pretty, and even shorter than Barrie; she laughed at his jokes; he also found that he could talk seriously to her. By 1893, their engagement was being assumed in London, but neither would admit the rumours, both dithered, no announcement came. Then in 1894, Barrie went home to visit his mother and caught pneumonia. While his life was in danger, newspapers printed daily reports on his condition and Mary Ansell left the cast of his play to go north to nurse him.

They were married at his mother's house in July 1894. Barrie's notebook entries two days before the wedding read: 'Boy all nerves. "You are very ignorant." How? Must we instruct you in the mysteries of love-making?'

On honeymoon in Switzerland, the follow-up is an idea for a play: 'Wife: Have you given me up? Have nothing to do with me? Husband calmly kind, no passion &c (a la self).'

Barrie, like Lear and Carroll, and also like Kenneth Grahame, was a bachelor by temperament. Years later, after *Peter Pan* and his divorce, he was sometimes mocked as 'the boy who couldn't go up'. It is doubtful whether his marriage was consummated; there were no children although Mary was desperate for them, and it was clear from the start that Barrie could not accept his role as husband. The books he wrote in the early years of married life – *Margaret Ogilvy*, a biography of his mother, and *Sentimental Tommy*, a novel about his own childhood – suggest an imaginative escape into the past. Then came *Tommy and Grizel* in 1900, a sequel in which Tommy grows up, and a *roman à clef* about Barrie's own marriage which pointed the way to *Peter Pan*.

Tommy, like Barrie a Scotsman and successful writer, grows from an imaginative and beloved child to a fantasising adult who believes his own role-plays so completely that he cannot separate them from reality; working on a story about a cripple, for instance, he develops a limp, persuades sympathetic friends and himself of actual wounds, and ends up with a sprained ankle. Equally taken by the romantic part of lover to his childhood friend Grizel, he marries her but remains 'a boy who could not with years become a man':

> Oh is it not cruel to ask a boy to love? . . . . He did not love her. 'Not as I love him', she said to herself. 'Not as married people ought to love'. . . . He was a boy who could not grow up.

Tommy fails at the role, the marriage is a catastrophe, and a final line, deleted from the manuscript before publication, hints at the sterility for which Barrie, at least subconsciously, admits responsibility: 'She lived so long after Tommy that she was almost a middle-aged woman when she died. What God will find hardest to forgive him, I think, is that Grizel never had a child.'

Deprived of children, the couple acquired an enormous St Bernard who was bigger than either of them and was named Porthos after the St Bernard in George du Maurier's novel *Peter Ibbetson*. Barrie's daily routine in the late 1890s included a lone walk with Porthos in Kensington Gardens, and it was here that his romance with other people's children began. Among the upper-class children who spent afternoons out with Nanny at the Gardens was a bold and charming boy of about four, with black curly hair, big eyes, a rosebud mouth and a bright red tam o'shanter. He was called George Llewelyn Davies, he came with his younger brother Jack, he played games with the writer and his dog, and Barrie became obsessed by him.

Some months after he started meeting George every day, Barrie went at the end of 1897 to a New Year's Eve dinner party for seventy-two guests. He was placed next to a beautiful, silent woman who at the end gathered up the after-dinner sweets into her handbag. Barrie asked why, and she said the sweets were 'for Peter'. It was then revealed that Peter was the brother of George and Jack, that she was Sylvia Llewelyn Davies, wife of a young barrister called Arthur, and that George was named for her father, George du Maurier, after whose fictional St Bernard Barrie called the dog that had first led him to Kensington Gardens. The du Maurier–Llewelyn Davies families were among the most glittering, well-connected and talented in London, and Barrie, the ambitious artist locked in a dull marriage, was hooked.

By the time Barrie wrote *Peter Pan*, the Llewelyn Davieses had five sons, George, Jack, Peter, Michael and Nico. Both Arthur and Sylvia were known for their striking good looks, grace and charm, which all the children inherited, and their Kensington home, warm, lively and shambling in the Bohemian du Maurier style, was to Barrie a haven. He adored

Sylvia, who shared his artistic interests and tastes – George du Maurier's novels such as *Trilby* have the same soft-focus appeal as Barrie's; her attraction was also her openly passionate love for her husband, which made Barrie feel safe as a platonic admirer. Her sons were living versions of his ideal of boyhood, with George, who had sparked his romance with the family, and Michael, the first brother he had known from birth, his clear favourites. With Arthur he had a difficult relationship, marred by jealousy and misunderstanding on both sides, but nothing could keep Barrie away. He became an over-frequent visitor and close friend; soon the Barries were taking holidays with the Llewelyn Davieses and Barrie regularly took the boys out for games or to the theatre.

Today a neighbour would catch one glimpse of the intense little writer playing with the boys and social workers would be on the Kensington doorstep in minutes. But whatever his fantasies, Barrie's behaviour seems to have been innocent – Nico later swore to Barrie's biographer Andrew Birkin that there was no hint of homosexuality or paedophilia; Barrie was simply sexless. Instead, he played out his reveries in a novel *The Little White Bird*, a second *roman à clef* which works through his relations with George.

The Little White Bird is the story of a childless writer, Captain W, who secretly helps a couple with a young child, David. He pretends he too has a son, Timothy, and when they fall on hard times, he tells them Timothy has died and gives them all his clothes. But in a rerun of the fantasy/reality world of Barrie's earlier *alter ego*, Tommy, the Captain so believes in his son that he mourns the death, which for Barrie becomes at once an elegy for the end of boyhood and a rapturous evocation of George. It is a quintessential piece of Edwardian writing on childhood:

> I wished (so had the phantasy of Timothy taken posses-sion of me) that before he went he could have played once in the Kensington Gardens, and have ridden on the fallen trees, calling gloriously to me to look; that he could have sailed one paper galleon on the Round Pond; fain would I

have had him chase one hoop a little way down the laughing avenues of childhood, where memory tells us we run but once, on a long summer day, emerging at the other end as men and women with all the fun to pay for.

After Timothy's 'death', the Captain grows obsessed with David, and plots to win him away from his mother, 'take him utterly from her and make him mine'. There are shades of Nabokovian sadism in his designs — he sends the mother a photo of David being hanged on a tree — and the climax is a bedtime scene oozing sexual fantasy:

> At twenty-five past six I turned on the hot water in the bath, and covertly swallowed a small glass of brandy. I then said, 'Half-past six; time for little boys to be in bed'. I said it in the matter-of-fact voice . . . as if there was nothing particularly delicious to me in hearing myself say it. . . .
>
> I cannot proceed in public with the disrobing of David.
>
> Soon the night nursery was in darkness but for the glimmer from the night-light, and very still save when the door creaked as a man peered in at the little figure on the bed. . . .
>
> 'What can it be, David?'
>
> 'I don't take up very much room', the far-away voice said.
>
> 'Why, David,' said I, sitting up, 'do you want to come into my bed?'
>
> 'Mother said I wasn't to want it unless you wanted it first', he squeaked.
>
> 'It is what I have been wanting all the time', said I, and then without more ado the little white figure rose and flung itself at me. For the rest of the night he lay on me and across me, and sometimes his feet were at the bottom of the bed and sometimes on the pillow, but he always retained possession of my finger, and occasionally he woke me to say that he was sleeping with me. I had not a good night. I lay thinking.
>
> Of this little boy, who, in the midst of his play while I undressed him, had suddenly buried his head on my knees. . . .

This is Barrie at his most sentimental yet psychologically acute on the adult's nervous knowingness versus the child's vulnerability. He probably intended romantic rather than sexual frisson. Yet both are there, and it is impossible now to read this passage without an echo of the self-mocking Humbert first seducing Lolita in an oddly similar situation half a century later:

> Upon hearing her first morning yawn, I feigned handsome profiled sleep. I just did not know what to do. Would she be shocked at finding me by her side, and not in some spare bed? Would she collect her clothes and lock herself up in the bathroom? . . . . I gave a mediocre imitation of waking up. . . . All at once, with a burst of rough glee (the sign of the nymphet!) she put her mouth to my ear – but for quite a while my mind could not separate into words the hot thunder of her whisper, and she laughed, and brushed the hair off her face, and tried again, and gradually the odd sense of living in a brand new, mad new dream world, where everything was permissible, came over me. . . .

The Little White Bird was published in 1902 and was so popular that Barrie was regularly accosted by mothers and sons in Kensington Gardens. Of particular interest was a story within the book, which the Captain tells David, about Peter Pan, a boy/fairy whose role is to bury dead children who break the rules by staying in the Gardens overnight. It was based on a tale Barrie made up for George, in which his baby brother Peter could fly out of his pram like a bird, and in *The Little White Bird* it emerges as Barrie's revenge fantasy on the parents he knew he could not emulate: 'But how strange for parents, when they hurry into the Gardens at the opening of the gates looking for their lost one, to find the sweetest little tombstone instead. I do hope that Peter is not too ready with his spade. It is all rather sad.'

On holiday with the Llewelyn Davies family in 1901, the other part of *Peter Pan* was invented in a six-week-long game of pirates, Indians and islands which Barrie at his most jubilant acted out with the boys around the lake and forest near his

Sussex cottage. He recast an island as a South Sea lagoon where the boys were marooned, himself as a pirate, Captain Swarthy, who made them walk the gangplank, and his dog as a tiger in a papier mâché mask. He was photographer as well as director, and later published privately an account of the summer with photos of the boys as heroes, called *The Boy Castaways of Black Lake Island* and purporting to be written by Peter Llewelyn Davies. Only two copies were printed; one was given to the boys' father, who immediately, probably intentionally, left it on a train.

Some of the *Black Lake* scenario appeared in the adult play *The Admirable Crichton* (1902), where the social hierarchy of a household is turned upside down when it is wrecked on an island, with the butler becoming chief. But the germ of a children's play already possessed Barrie. He was now over forty and the pattern of his life was fixed: he was a literary celebrity but an emotional outsider who derived his sustenance from another man's family, idealised his mother and was unable either to relate to his wife or produce his own children. Into *Peter Pan* poured the dreams, dashed hopes and terrors which had always haunted him.

Peter Pan is a wish-fulfilment story about the triumph of youth over age which caught the mood of the new young century. One of Barrie's favourite books was *Coral Island*, and in *Peter Pan* he turns the traditional swash-buckling sea dream (*Robinson Crusoe*, *The Swiss Family Robinson*) into a play for the times. It is the story of a fairy/god/boy figure, Peter Pan, who enters the nursery of the Darling children, Wendy, John and Michael, and teaches them to fly. The Darling children have a loving mother, a cruel father and a nurse who is an English sheepdog. One night, when she is locked up, they fly away with Peter to his wild island, Neverland. Wendy becomes mother to a group of lost boys, 'children who fall out of their perambulators when the nurse is looking the other way', and their adventures include battles with Indians, pirates led by the terrible Captain Hook, and a crocodile who ticks relentlessly because he has swallowed a clock. They nearly die when Hook captures them, but as they are about to walk the gangplank on his ship, Peter fights Hook and kicks him into the sea, where he is eaten by the crocodile. The children return home, the Darling parents adopt the lost boys, but Peter refuses to join them and remains always a boy in Neverland.

Framed by Edwardian domesticity, inspired by the Edwardian ideals of youth and the great outdoors, sentimental and dated, *Peter Pan* has nevertheless a magical, symbolical quality that makes it a masterpiece. Almost a century after it was written, Peter Pan remains a byword for eternal youth. The crocodile is one of the most original images of devouring Time in literature. Neverland, the wendy house, the lost boys, all have a deep and lasting resonance. Written to be performed at Christmas like a traditional pantomime, which is based on folk tales like *Puss in Boots* or *Jack in the Beanstalk*, it contains too the archetypes of the fairy story – the children-heroes (Peter Pan and Wendy) and the villain (Hook). And the fantasy setting – the Neverland island with the Mermaid's Lagoon, the Marooner's Rock, the neverbirds – is an enchanted, other world or dream reality as heady and attractive as any in children's literature.

The mix of ingredients is unique. On the one hand, here is the boys' adventure story laced with dreams of military glory – 'We hope our sons will die like English gentlemen', says Wendy. On the other, the story is a fantasy filled with imaginings both elegiac and erotic. The combination recalls the poems of Barrie's contemporary Housman, with their nostalgic, patriotic versions of the country idyll, yet *Peter Pan* is also playful, upbeat and breathes the warmth of the people and day-to-day games and pleasures that Barrie loved. The boys take their names and characters from the Llewelyn Davies children; Wendy, an invented name, is named after W. E. Henley's daughter Margaret, who called Barrie 'my friendy', which with a lisp came out as 'wendy'. Nana is Barrie's dog, and Mrs Darling, 'the loveliest lady in Bloomsbury', is Sylvia, the mother Barrie idealised after his own. Mr Darling is not

Arthur, although Barrie would have liked Arthur to be as unsympathetic, but the more powerful symbol of every father figure that a child wants to vanquish.

Traditionally, Mr Darling and Captain Hook are played by the same actor; both are sexually mature male villains over whom the child Peter and the Lost Boys triumph. Hook, characterised by phallic symbolism from the start – the iron hook which twitches involuntarily, the big cigar – is a powerfully sexual creature who tries to seduce Wendy away from the boys. She finds him fascinating as well as frightening; for Barrie too he is attractive – he called him 'thou not wholly unheroic figure'. In the first performances, Gerald du Maurier, the Llewelyn Davies boys' actor-uncle, played him so compellingly that children were hauled screaming from the theatre; his daughter, Daphne du Maurier, recalled how he caught the essence of childhood fears and desires:

> He was a tragic and rather ghastly creation who knew no peace, and whose soul was in torment; a dark shadow; a sinister dream; a bogey of fear who lives perpetually in the grey recesses of every small boy's mind. All boys had their Hooks, as Barrie knew; he was the phantom who came by night and stole his way into their murky dreams.[10]

Yet Hook, for all his sexual charisma, is a marked man, pursued by Time in the figure of the ever-ticking crocodile, doomed to age and die while Peter crows in victory 'I'm youth, I'm joy'. Mr Darling, Peter's other adult rival, is also defeated, this time by ridicule. He is an early hero of the Theatre of the Absurd who spends the play in a dog kennel, to atone for the fact that he locked up the dog-nurse and thus let his children escape.

Sexual repression, a hint of child sexuality bubbling under the surface, is a driving force in *Peter Pan*. Like Barrie's other heroes, the failed husband Tommy and the non-father Captain W, Peter Pan is a character close to Barrie himself, but transplanted to the context of a children's fantasy where his youth and sexual immaturity triumph. Peter rejects the advances of Tiger Lily, Tinker Bell, through whom sexuality is

Mabel Lucie Attwell's drawing of Mr Darling, the vanquished father-figure: 'In the bitterness of his remorse he swore that he would never leave the kennel until his children came back.'

portrayed as wanton decadence, and Wendy. Their first encounter has a whiff of sex – he teaches her to fly, a symbol of eroticism, and she tries to touch and kiss him. But while she matures sexually, he remains a boy, repeating the pattern of Barrie's Tommy and Grizel:

> WENDY (*She is too loving to be ignorant that he is not loving enough, and she hesitates like one who knows the answer to her question.*) What is wrong, Peter?
> PETER (*scared*). It is only pretend, isn't it, that I am their father?
> WENDY (*drooping*). Oh, yes. (*His sigh of relief is without consideration for her feelings.*) But they are ours, Peter, yours and mine.
> PETER (*determined to get at facts, the only things that puzzle him*). But not really?
> WENDY. Not if you don't wish it.
> PETER. I don't.
> WENDY (*knowing she ought not to probe but driven to it by something within*). What are your exact feelings for me, Peter?
> PETER (*in the class-room*). Those of a devoted son, Wendy.
> WENDY (*turning away*). I thought so.

Wendy is left a Virgin Mother; with Mrs Darling, she joins a group of idealised but sexually unthreatening mother-figures who appear in English fiction for the next two decades – Shaw's Candida; Mrs Wilcox in Forster's *Howard's End*; Mrs Ramsay in *To the Lighthouse*; in nostalgic throwback, Lady Marchmain in *Brideshead Revisited*.[11] Wendy is the most innocent of them, while Peter is confirmed as Pan, god of boyhood:

> WENDY (*making a last attempt*). You don't feel you would like to say anything to my parents, Peter, about a very sweet subject?
> PETER. No, Wendy.
> WENDY. About me, Peter?
> PETER. No. (*He gets out his pipes, which she knows is a very bad sign.*)

Peter pipes his way off to the fantasy world of Neverland, 'so no one is as gay as he'. But through the whimsical charm is streaked a terrible awareness of what really happens, as Barrie knew, when a boy will not grow up. Peter Pan is lonely – 'No one must ever touch me' – confused, doomed to exile. Barrie's biographer Denis Mackail, who, aged twelve, saw Nina Boucicault as the first Peter, confirms that what brought the character to life from the start was this tragic quality:

> Miss Boucicault was the Peter of all Peters . . . . She was unearthly but she was real. She obtruded neither sex nor sexlessness, which has so far beaten everyone else. Above all she had the touch of heart-breaking tragedy that is there in the story or fable from beginning to end.[12]

'To be born is to be wrecked on an island', Barrie wrote in an introduction to *Coral Island*. Loneliness was a condition of his life and of his major characters, from Tommy and Captain W to the butler Crichton, Peter Pan, Hook ('he was so terribly alone') and his late heroine Mary Rose. His best plays have island settings, and he echoed Edward Lear in seeing them as places of exile as well as escape. In *Peter Pan and Wendy*, the novel version of the play published in 1911, the Lost Boys are comically written off into conventional adults, with the stupidest, Tootles, ironically becoming a judge. But tragedy belongs to Peter Pan, who cannot join the crowd and remains the outsider looking in at the happily reunited Darling family: 'He had ecstasies innumerable that other children can never know; but he was looking through the window at the one joy from which he must be for ever barred.'

Years later, Barrie fully realised that in Peter Pan he had drawn himself, the outsider looking in at the Llewelyn Davies family. In 1922, aged sixty-two, he noted, 'It is as if long after writing *Peter Pan* its true meaning came to me – desperate attempt to grow up but can't.'[13] His fantasy, like those of Lear, Carroll and the others, is tinged with the sadness and truth of a frustrated life.

Barrie's fixations – on boyhood, mothers, other people's

families – had free reign in *Peter Pan*, and so personally engrossed in the play did he become that for once he distrusted his commercial judgement. He offered it to his producer, the flamboyant American Charles Frohman, over lunch at the Garrick Club with the following proposal: 'I am sure it will not be a commercial success. But it is a dream-child of mine, and I am so anxious to see it on the stage that I have written another play which I will be glad to give you and which will compensate you for any loss on the one I am so eager to see produced.' But Frohman fell headlong for the play, changing only the title, from 'The Great White Father', and leaving instructions that Barrie was to have all the funds he wanted for a spectacular Christmas opening.

Back in New York, Frohman was so excited that he would stop friends in the street and act out scenes from the play. In London Barrie was by 1904 a crowd-pulling name, and rumours about a long-awaited new play were rife, but rehearsals were held in secret, the cast had scripts only of their own parts, and few knew the plot. When the actress Hilda Trevelyan turned up for her first day's rehearsal as Wendy, she was told to get her life insured and then start a two-week 'flying' course with George Kirkby's Flying Ballet Company. A special flying harness was invented for the play, but many of Barrie's mechanical effects had to be axed at the last minute because they were so complicated. Barrie held up rehearsals for the Llewelyn Davies boys to visit the theatre and fly about the stage, and eventually the pre-Christmas opening was postponed. Barrie spent Christmas Day 1904 rewriting the last scene, rehearsals continued through the night on Boxing Day because the stage hands refused to work on Christmas Day, and throughout, the confidence of cast and author waned. Barrie later recalled that during rehearsals 'a depressed man in overalls carrying a mug of tea or a paint-pot, used often to appear by my side in the shadowy stalls and say to me "The gallery boys won't stand it." '[14]

On the day, Barrie, panicking about the response to the lines 'Do you believe in fairies? Say quick that you believe! If you believe, clap your hands!' arranged with the orchestra that they should clap if necessary. Frohman, at home in New York on the snowy afternoon of 27 December, acted out the whole play himself, getting down on all fours to play Nana and the crocodile, as he waited for a cable with a verdict on the opening. Eventually, delayed by a snowstorm, it came: '*Peter Pan* all right. Looks like a big success.'

From its first night, *Peter Pan* was a hit. With no idea of what to expect, an audience of mostly adults thrilled with amazement when the curtain rose, clapped so boisterously about their belief in fairies that Nina Boucicault as Peter burst into tears, and screamed for curtain-calls long into the evening. The critics loved it, children begged to go to matinée after matinée, aficionados took up places in the front stalls to throw thimbles at Peter and jeer Hook, and Barrie became more famous, and richer, than ever. *Peter Pan* is still one of the most popular plays written this century.

Barrie lived more than thirty years after *Peter Pan*, but he never produced anything as successful again. In 1911 he rewrote the play as a novel; there followed minor works, but nothing important until the play *Mary Rose* in 1920. In the interval, Barrie had little time or need to write; instead, the story of *Peter Pan* began to come true.

The year the play opened, the Llewelyn Davieses moved twenty-five miles out of London to a rambling old house at Berkhamsted. Barrie's involvement might have tapered off, but soon the family's country idyll was shattered. In 1906, Arthur Llewelyn Davies was diagnosed as having cancer of the jaw, and Barrie became a source of invaluable emotional and practical care. He had always been mesmerised by the bond between Sylvia and Arthur, as well as excluded by it; now he felt acutely with them both. Old jealousies were irrelevant, he grew close to Arthur in the last year, he helped Sylvia, and gave assurances of financial support. By 1907, after a year of horrible operations which left him unable to speak, Arthur was dead.

Worse was to come. Sylvia never really recovered from Arthur's death, and though she struggled on for her children,

she also became ill and too weak to move from her bedroom. Barrie, watching his model family fall apart, was devastated. He had been living an increasingly separate life from his wife, was divorced in 1909 – the grounds were Mary's infidelity – and now occupied himself almost entirely with this tragic household. His first protégé George was away at Eton and sent cheery letters home, but the younger boys suffered greatly, especially Michael, the most sensitive and Barrie's favourite. Gerald du Maurier recalled visiting Sylvia on her sickbed and noticing the tiny figure of Michael, aged ten, doing his homework in the corner of her room with tears silently streaming down his face.

In 1910 Sylvia died, leaving her mother, brothers and Barrie as joint guardians of five boys aged from seven to seventeen, but requesting that they should not be split up. It was obvious that only Barrie had both time and money to care for them all together. The will also suggested that 'Jenny', a sister of the boys' nanny and housekeeper, might move into the family home to help. Barrie, copying out the will, transcribed this as 'Jimmy', the family's name for him, and his authority was assured. A few years after *Peter Pan*, Barrie's life was transformed: from an unhappily married oddball looking into other lives, he became a single, boyish man in charge of five lost boys – as close to a live, adult version of Peter as could be imagined.

Barrie poured his energy into caring for this inherited family. *Peter Pan* continued to haunt them. Peter, beginning at Eton, was mocked as the 'real' Peter Pan. Michael, highly strung and most affected by the loss of his parents – Nico was too young, the others found some escape away at school – had nightmares of boys flying in through the window to fetch him. Barrie used to sit through the night reassuring and consoling him, and Michael became passionately dependent on his guardian. Barrie's biographer Denis Mackail, who knew them at this time, wrote of their desperately close relationship; when Michael started at Eton in 1913, he was so lonely and unhappy that only Barrie's frequent letters could revive him. They wrote to each other every day, and when Michael left Eton, by then the most charming and popular boy in the school, there was a stack of more than 2,000 letters which had sustained him. The teenage Michael also became Barrie's most trusted literary critic, judging manuscripts which awaited his arrival on vacation, and accompanying Barrie to *Peter Pan* rehearsals at Christmas.

Worldly success continued to follow Barrie. He was made a baronet in 1913, and when he tried to visit America quietly in 1914, every word he said, from 'Barrie says War Will be Long' to 'Barrie Likes our Virginia Ham', was pasted on billboards, and he was invited to stay with Roosevelt. But the tragedies and responsibilities since *Peter Pan* were taking their toll. A photograph of the Allahakbarries Cricket Team in 1905 shows a youthful-looking Barrie, then forty-five, in holiday mood, holding on to Michael as a mascot. Eight years later, the last Allahakbarrie team, including George Llewelyn Davies, now a handsome young man, and the young playwright A. A. Milne, was photographed in 1913 and shows Barrie, fifty-three, already an old man, face lined and drawn, body hunched, the most tense and sad figure of the group.

In 1914, George and Peter, both Cambridge under-graduates, signed up as second-lieutenants when war was declared; Jack continued at naval college and then joined the Navy. Barrie wrote a propaganda play, *Der Tag*, in which the German Emperor debates with the spirit of Culture. His first intensely-felt loss in the fighting was Guy du Maurier, Sylvia's brother, who for him epitomised the famous du Maurier charm that he recreated in many of his characters:

> He certainly had the du Maurier charm at its best – the light heart with the sad smile, & it might be the sad heart with the bright smile. He had lots of stern stuff in him, and yet always the mournful smile of one who could pretend that life was gay but knew it wasn't.[15]

This was written in 1915, in the last letter to reach George Llewelyn Davies alive. In his grief and worry, it continues as something like a love letter:

I do seem to be sadder today than ever, and more and more wishing you were a girl of 21 instead of a boy, so that I could say the things to you that are now always in my heart. For four years I have been waiting for you to become 21 & a little more, so that we could get closer & closer to each other, without any words needed. I don't have any little iota of desire for you to get military glory . . . but I have the one passionate desire that we may all be together again once at least. . . . I have lost all sense I ever had of war being glorious, it is just unspeakably monstrous to me now.

Four days after the letter was written, George was killed in Flanders. He had been adored by all who knew him, and for his contemporaries he was an emblem of the young man killed at the peak of his promise, the type of whom Housman had written prophetically two decades earlier. 'Few that survive would recall anyone whose image serves better as the flower and type of that doomed generation . . . the bloom of youth on them still . . . too young to have been coarsened', his brother wrote.[16]

For Barrie, George had started off both *Peter Pan* and his romance with the real lost boys, and his death was the third and worst personal catastrophe in a decade. But like a haunted man, he could not give up the dream of eternal youth, however hollow that ideal now appeared. Later, Charles Frohman, his producer and the man who had first had faith in *Peter Pan*, was killed travelling to see him when the *Lusitania* was torpedoed by German U-boats. Frohman refused a place in a lifeboat saying, 'Why fear death? It is the greatest adventure in life', which last words Barrie was soon retelling as, 'To die will be an awfully big adventure', although that line was actually cut from the play in 1915.

Again and again now Barrie rewrote life in terms of his own fantasy. He was, for example, godfather to Captain Scott's son Peter, named after Peter Pan, and was a supportive guardian after Scott died in 1913. But by 1922 Scott's death, too, had become a variation on the favourite theme, and Barrie told it as a fairy tale of a mountaineer who died young but reappeared years later still a youth:

> Some of the survivors returned to the glacier to see if the prediction would be fulfilled; all old men now; and the body reappeared as young as on the date he left them. So Scott and his comrades emerge out of the white immensities, always young.[17]

In a cruel paradox, the man whose fantasy came partly true grew unable to see actual tragedy in terms other than romantic myth, like his fantasist heroes Tommy, Captain W and Peter Pan, whose life is conditioned by an absolute failure to distinguish truth from make-believe:

> PETER (*passionately*). I want always to be a little boy and to have fun. (*So perhaps he thinks, but it is only his greatest pretend.*)

When the war ended, the youngest Llewelyn Davies son was almost grown up, and Barrie was more or less alone. As he began work on a new play, he developed an acute cramp in his right arm and it became quite useless, a strange parallel to Captain Hook's iron claw and also an expression of his own withered emotions. He taught himself to write with his left hand, which became his excuse for the 'darker and more sinister outlook on life' in his work, and wrote his last great play, *Mary Rose*.

When *Mary Rose* opened in 1920, many thought it Barrie's best play; although scarcely performed now, it is a skilfully dramatic work, and full of insights into Barrie's battle with the idea of youth and age. Mary Rose's parents cannot bear her to grow up, and when she is eleven their wish is cruelly granted: she disappears, presumed drowned, off an island in the Hebrides similar to those where Barrie spent holidays with the Llewelyn Davies boys. But twenty days later she turns up, unaware that she has been missing. She never properly matures and when she marries, becomes a girl-wife in the mould of Wendy. Her terror is that she and her husband will grow old and that her baby son must grow up. She disappears again, this time for twenty-five years, and returns still a young woman, to find all has changed terrifyingly: a middle-aged husband and elderly parents are dazed by her arrival, and her beloved baby has grown up. In the last act, she is dead but returns as a ghost, still childish, still demanding her baby, and losing her memory and her sense of identity. Like Barrie, she is haunted by the past, obsessed by a lost son; she is also the child who cannot grow up, who must watch everyone around her maturing while she cannot, and the victim of her own fantasies which come true in a horrible manner.

There was one last twist in the wheel of truth and fiction in Barrie's life. A year after *Mary Rose*, in 1921, Michael, the most loved and gifted of his adopted sons, actually was drowned in a bathing accident in Oxford with his best friend Rupert Buxton. Barrie had been terrified by the distance Michael had been putting between them since he had become an undergraduate, in an obvious effort to break away with occasional lapses into intimacy. Michael was temperamental, given to depression, had thought about fleeing Oxford for Paris. Barrie knew he had been most scarred from the early loss of his parents. There were strong rumours that the deaths were suicide, a mutual pact, and of a homosexual relationship between Michael and Buxton; witnesses had seen them not struggling but merely clasping each other in the water.

'I am sure if he had lived he would have been one of the remarkable people of his generation', wrote Lytton Strachey.[18] Fellow undergraduates howled at his funeral; friends wrote hysterical letters to each other. Like George's, Michael's death at twenty-one shocked a wide circle of contemporaries. He too became something of a mythical figure, and one of a number of young men who had missed the war but died 'accidental' deaths, or committed suicide, in the years immediately following it. A subconscious cause, maybe, was their guilt at not having participated in the fight that had seen many of their peers killed. Kenneth Grahame's twenty-year-old son Alastair, who made his suicide look like an accident on a railway line, died exactly a year before Michael, also at Oxford. Each was born in 1900, each had been the centre of hope and love of a great children's writer, and each had grown up in the shadow of masterpieces for and about childhood which had fixed the mood of the Edwardian age. In a sense, they were as much victims of the cult of glorious youth as the war-time casualties; young men suffused in a personal sense by the dream of eternal boyhood, boys to whom Barrie and Grahame transferred their own ideals of childhood, and for whom adulthood then seemed impossible to face.

Barrie had survived the other losses, but he was finished by Michael's death. For days he shut himself away and would see no one, not even Nico, and there were fears that he too would kill himself. 'All the world is different to me now. Michael was pretty much my world,' he wrote.[19] Michael looked out from every young face he saw, he had dreams where Michael returned and he could not prevent his impending death, and he thought about him every day. Photographs after 1921 show a man much older than Barrie's sixty years; he is bent, beaten down and wizened; his secretary Cynthia Asquith wrote that he 'looked like a man in a nightmare'. His eyes in late photographs have a dazed, staring expression, and he became, like his mother half a century before and like his latest heroine, a ghost living half in the past with his dead son. The title of his last play, *The Boy David* (1936), still recalled the boy brother whose death had first imprinted on Barrie the idea of eternal youth.

He lived alone in London, a changed and darkened man. Gradually he emerged and spent his last years seeing friends, and continuing an effortless haul of worldly trophies. He became Chancellor of Edinburgh University, and was awarded the Order of Merit. In old age a new generation of child-friends included Princess Margaret, who aged three announced that he 'is my greatest friend, and I am his greatest friend'. He died in London in 1937. More than twenty years later, Peter Llewelyn Davies threw himself under a train at Sloane Square station, the third untimely death of Barrie's five lost boys. He had suffered all his life as the namesake of Peter Pan, and in middle age he still called the play 'that terrible masterpiece'.

5

Kenneth Grahame
Et in Arcadia Ego

You *like* people. They interest you. But I am
interested in *places*.

Kenneth Grahame
to his wife

'I mourn the safe and motherly old middle class queen, who held the nation warm under the fold of her big hideous Scotch-plaid shawl',[1] wrote Henry James when Queen Victoria died in 1901. Victorian fantasies are as cluttered and claustrophobic as a dark, frilly nineteenth-century drawing room – Alice at the bottom of a rabbit hole, the Water Babies under the seabed, Lear's sugar tongs and nutcrackers and five pound notes. Their settings are often subterranean caverns or domestic prisons – the night-kingdom in George MacDonald's *The Day Boy and the Night Girl*, the chaotic children's party in Christina Rossetti's *Speaking Likenesses*. But around 1900 the landscape of children's books opens out, to the wide vistas of Grahame's Arcadian river bank and Barrie's exotic island, to the rural lanes and villages of Beatrix Potter's Peter Rabbit tales and to the idyllic country estate of Frances Hodgson Burnett's *The Secret Garden*. Both *The Wind in the Willows* and *Peter Pan* begin with a deliberate flight up and out into the open, from Mole's underground home to the river, out of John and Wendy's nursery into the sky. A characteristic of Edwardian children's books was to mix romantic exploration of a great outdoors and boyish high spirits with Victorian sentimentality and wish-fulfilment. The resulting backcloth of a lush, sun-dappled Edwardian summer is nowhere so perfectly distilled as in Grahame's nostalgic account:

> They recalled the languorous siesta of hot mid day, deep in green undergrowth, the sun striking through in tiny golden shafts and spots; the boating and bathing of the afternoon, the rambles along dusty lanes and through

yellow cornfields; and the long cool evening at last, when
so many threads were gathered up, so many friendships
rounded, and so many adventures planned for the
morrow.

Like Barrie's, Kenneth Grahame's life and work illustrates
the changes in the perception of childhood since Carroll and
Alice. In particular, Grahame, as a bachelor with a taste for
country pursuits, experienced to its height the 1890s life of the
eternal boy – the kinship between men, the boating and
picnicking and walking parties, the occasional adventuring, the
lazy bonhomie. He knew at first hand the lives of the boyish
hedonists who are the group heroes of both *The Wind in the
Willows* and *Peter Pan*.

Where the Victorians had escaped into a fantastical vision of
childhood for solace and distraction, the Edwardians went one
stage further and attempted to play at childhood in their own
adult lives. The fashions of the day were for the great outdoors:
for hearty, tweed-clad men smoking pipes, tramping across the
Downs, for plunging into cold rivers, disciplining boys,
shooting animals and building empires; among Edwardian
legacies are Baden-Powell's boy scouts (he called them 'boy-
men') and garden cities. And the intellectual climate was
transformed: as the moral and theological debates of the old
century dissolved, in their place came a hazy desire for
spirituality which gives Edwardian writing its peculiar quality
of secular earnestness. It came closest to a religion in the
worship of nature and a fascination for Pan, the god of nature
who was half-boy, half-beast. Such nature-worship con-
veniently twisted nineteenth-century legacies – Ruskinian
reverence for God-in-nature, sentimental portrayals of
children – into Edwardian dreams of eternal playfulness, the
hint of fulfilment through pleasure rather than restraint. Pan
haunted Edwardian writers from Barrie and Grahame to
Kipling, Forster, George Moore and D. H. Lawrence.

In this climate, the anarchic mid-Victorian fantasy was
tamed into something more familiar and children's writing
joined the mainstream literary tradition. The popularity and

importance of Victorian children's books had lain in their ability to challenge the mainstream from outside. Carroll and Lear were eccentric loners, and, as a mathematician and an artist, significantly men outside the literary establishment, who pioneered a new genre. By contrast the next generation of children's writers, typified by Barrie and Grahame, were successful authors who made their names with a subject that was all the rage, stories for adults about childhood, and then wrote a children's classic. They were the products of a culture already suffused with the theme of youth.

It is said that ladies' hats traditionally get larger before a war; the same drive to escape, to grab pleasure while there was time, inspired Edwardian children's writers, and made them more popular than ever. The two decades before 1914 were the age when everyone wanted to read about a golden world of children romping across the countryside. Sentimental collections like Robert Louis Stevenson's *A Child's Garden of Verses* and Walter de la Mare's *Songs of Childhood* were loved by adults. Kenneth Grahame's stories about childhood, *Dream Days* and *The Golden Age*, were bestsellers and famous exports advertising the contemporary English Eden. *The Golden Age* was the only book in addition to the Bible that Kaiser William II kept on the pleasure yacht where he spent his summers, and Theodore Roosevelt was so fond of both Grahame's collections that he demanded autographed copies and invited their author to the White House. To anyone looking at Britain from outside, the ideal of a child-centred Arcadian idyll was deeply interwoven into the imaginative life of the country.

Kenneth Grahame, like J. M. Barrie, was born a mid-Victorian and a Scotsman, and grew up when British culture was already fixated on childhood. Like Barrie, he never let go of the ideal of childhood, and his personal life was bound up with the irrepressibly boyish characters of his writing. Within a more orthodox shell than Barrie's, and from the framework of an apparently conventional job and marriage, Grahame too was the typical Edwardian boy-man who could not grow up.

He was born in 1859, the third child in a wealthy Edinburgh family. He grew up within sight of Inverary Castle and Lock Fyne; his father, indolent but well-connected, was Sheriff-Substitute of Argyllshire, and his beautiful, talented mother used to take her children to visit the Duchess of Argyll at the castle. But their charmed family life fell to pieces when Bessie Grahame died after the birth of her fourth child in 1864. Their father, unable to face the children, sent them at once south to live with their maternal grandmother in Berkshire, shut up his house and fled to France, where he died, an alcoholic, at Le Havre twenty years later. Grahame, like Lear, was always scarred by this early desertion. His books focus on homes lost and restored – in *The Wind and the Willows* the Rat, the Mole, the Toad, even the baby Otter are each driven by the desire to find or recover their homes – but not once in his writing does he mention parents. From the time he left Scotland for the south, he built up his defences and transferred his emotional allegiance to places, not people.

In Berkshire, Granny Ingles, an efficient if not affectionate guardian, lived in a graceful old hunting lodge, The Mount, which had once been on the edge of Windsor Forest but by the 1860s was surrounded by acres of gardens and orchards. The young Kenneth had little rapport with his formal, forbidding grandmother but he fell in love with her house, and with the lazy stretches of the Thames around Cookham and Pang-bourne, and the gently rolling countryside beyond. Deprived of sympathetic company, he spent days wandering, solitary and dreamy, along the river; later, the river consoled him when he was despatched to St Edward's School in Oxford, and he drew again on the same inner resources to cope with the hostile crowd. 'The barrack-like school, the arid, cheerless class-rooms, drove him to Nature for redress', he wrote in an autobiographical sketch in *Pagan Papers*. The persona of the lonely observer with a strong sense of place was already established: 'misty recollections of friends – clear and distinct of desk, stair, cistern, room', he remembered. He always felt most at home alone in the country – there are also parallels with

16. Thomas Gotch, *The Child Enthroned* (1894). Gotch's portrait of his daughter Hester was influenced by the style of Italian quattrocento religious paintings. Contemporary critics noted its 'almost Gothic conviction of feeling' and compared it to paintings of the Christ Child.

17. George Elgar Hicks, *A Cloud with a Silver Lining* (1890). In its suggestions of the dying child as both sacrificial victim and spiritual king, Hicks's picture recalls both a Pietà and an Adoration. Sentimentalised child death scenes such as that of Little Nell in Dickens's *The Old Curiosity Shop* and little William in Mrs H. Wood's *East Lynne*, which sold 400,000 copies from 1861 to 1895, were also very popular.

18. Kate Greenaway, *The Garden Seat* (*c.* 1890). Childhood is often associated with a beautiful enclosed garden in Victorian and Edwardian art. Kate Greenaway's innocent children had a wide following; devotees included John Ruskin, who begged her, unsuccessfully, to send him pictures of little girls wearing fewer clothes.

19. Henry Wallis, *Chatterton* (1856). By dying early, Thomas Chatterton was preserved in the public imagination as an idealised, eternally youthful romantic poet.

20. John Singer Sargent, *Portrait of Graham Robertson* (1894). Robertson was a friend of Kenneth Grahame, and a fashionable dandy in 1890s London. An aesthete and illustrator, he knew both Whistler and Oscar Wilde, and his looks have something in common with Wilde's ever-young dandy Dorian Gray.

21. Charles Sims, *The Beautiful is Fled* (*c.* 1900). A fascination with the faun, or Pan, half-human, half-beast, was widespread among the Edwardians. Sims's picture shares the wistfulness of the apparition of Pan in *The Wind in the Willows*.

22. Charles Spencelayh, *Dreams of Glory* (1900). This was painted during the Boer War; the child's patriotic dreams are close to those of Peter Pan and the lost boys, for whom 'to die will be an awfully big adventure'.

23. J. M. Barrie, aged thirty-five, in a photograph taken around the time of his marriage in 1894.

24. George, Jack and Peter Llewelyn Davies, aged eight, seven and four, playing pirates with Barrie during a holiday in 1901. Their make-believe adventures inspired the story of *Peter Pan*.

25. Kensington Gardens and the Round Pond, *c.* 1900, where J. M. Barrie first met George Llewelyn Davies. The stories he told the boy included one about Peter Pan flying round the Gardens. Kenneth Grahame's son Alastair also came here in the 1900s, but he was so unruly that the keeper made an official complaint about him.

26. The Allahakbarries, J. M. Barrie's cricket team, photographed in
1913. Included are: (*middle row, third left*) Barrie, (*middle row, first left*)
A. A. Milne, (*back row, first left*) George Llewelyn Davies and (*middle
row, second right*) Milne's publisher at Methuen, E. V. Lucas.

27. Kenneth Grahame in a portrait
by John Singer Sargent, 1912.

28. A. A. Milne in 1921, when he
was famous as a playwright.

29, 30, 31 and 32. Fathers and sons. (*above left*) Kenneth Grahame in old age and (*above right*) Alastair Grahame, to whom he first told *The Wind in the Willows*. (*below left*) J. V. Milne and his sons in 1886: four-year-old Alan, the youngest and the favourite, is seated. The boys are wearing the Little Lord Fauntleroy costume made popular by the book, published that year. (*below right*) A. A. Milne, his son Christopher and Winnie-the-Pooh, photographed by Howard Coster in 1926.

Edward Lear here. Many years later, Grahame's friend Graham Robertson recalled 'Oddly enough (for he was a most attractive man) Kenneth had few friends. He simply didn't want them. He would say rather wonderingly to his wife: "You *like* people. They interest you. But I am interested in *places*." '[2]

Grahame's school, St Edward's, was a second-rank establishment with an average batch of unenlightened Victorian masters but one redeeming feature: a level of disorganisation so great that, instead of games, the boys were allowed to wander around Oxford and the neighbouring villages outside lessons. By ten, Grahame knew every stone of the town and every bend in the river; he had fallen in love with a place that remained the Golden City of his imagination for the rest of his life. Nothing was ever so perfect again, and the fashionable paganism that came to mark his writing he always attributed to Oxford:

> The two influences which most soaked into me there, and have remained with me ever since, were the good grey Gothic on the one hand and, on the other, the cool secluded reaches of the Thames – the 'stripling Thames', remote and dragonfly haunted, before it attains to the noise, ribbons, and flannels of Folly Bridge. The education, in my time, was of the fine old crusted order. . . . But these elements, the classics, the Gothic, the primeval Thames, fostered in me, perhaps, the pagan germ. . . .[3]

Grahame was growing up in the Oxford of the 1870s, the city of theological passions and conversions and firebrand debates about aestheticism, the home of Arnold, Ruskin and also Lewis Carroll, who wrote *Through the Looking-Glass* when Grahame was a boy there. By the end of his schooldays, he saw the city as his spiritual home, and had he gone on to be an undergraduate, he would probably have become a mildly eccentric bachelor don like Carroll. But now came the second disappointment of his life: his sour Scottish Uncle John refused to support him at the university, and a clerkship at the Bank of England was found for him instead. Again banished from a place that had become home, to the orphan adolescent, dependent on the charity of relatives, the intellectual and literary life seemed to close before him for ever. For ten years, he could not bring himself to revisit Oxford.

But the Bank, like the school, proved to have virtues, as it were, by default. On his first day, 1 January 1879, Threadneedle Street was glumly shrouded in one of the dense, sickly yellow fogs that often occurred in Victorian London. Grahame took ninety minutes to walk there from his rooms in Bloomsbury, only to find the offices deserted. Hours later, bankers wandered in desultorily, explaining that a 'London Particular' was an excuse for a morning off. So relaxed was the working style that a relative once claimed the titles of Grahame's books *Dream Days* and *The Golden Age* to be directly inspired by life at the Bank. The books were certainly written during working hours, and although the Bank and the City did not stimulate Grahame, the work was not arduous, he was clever – at thirty-nine he became effortlessly the youngest Secretary the Bank had known – and it left him with ample leisure for long weekends in Berkshire, for a new addiction, travel to the south, especially to Italy, and for writing.

For twenty years, he lived as a London bachelor with sybaritic tastes and literary inclinations. He grew obsessive about Mediterranean food and became an aficionado of Italian restaurants in Soho. Photographs from this period show a large, handsome man with a wide face, dashing moustache, bushy eyebrows, an eager yet reserved expression, and the haunted, piercing look in the eyes which mark pictures of Grahame from childhood to old age. He had by all accounts a gentle, courteous manner, an easy humour, and though often solitary, was convivial and jocular in informal settings. Soon he was invited to the drawing rooms of writers and artists like W. E. Henley and Aubrey Beardsley; he joined walking and reading and smoking parties, and in 1893 he wrote his first book, *Pagan Papers*, extolling the pleasures of this sort of life. It was followed by two books about childhood, *The Golden Age* (1895) and *Dream Days* (1898), and by 1900 Grahame was internationally famous for three books which not one in a thousand readers of *The Wind in the Willows* today have even glimpsed.

'I wonder whether you would care to publish a quite small selection of articles that I have had in the *National Observer* and *St James's Gazette* during the past few years? They are, I think, just sufficiently individual and original to stand it' began a letter the publisher John Lane received from a diffident young man in 1893. Grahame's *Pagan Papers*, a slim, elegant volume, appeared at the end of the year with an illustration of a cheeky, fun-loving Pan by Aubrey Beardsley as the frontispiece. Beardsley's Pan, a typical Edwardian god, is charming, almost a dandy, dangerously attractive. But inside, in stories such as 'The Lost Centaur' and 'The Rural Pan', Pan is transplanted to Grahame's own imaginative Paradise; he is desexed, and he is already in the company of the characters who were to star in *The Wind in the Willows* fifteen years later.

> In solitudes such as these Pan sits and dabbles, and all the air is full of the music of his piping. . . . Out of hearing of all the clamour, the rural Pan may be found stretched on Ranmore Common, loitering under Abinger Pines, or prone by the secluded stream of the sinuous Mole, abounding in friendly greetings for his foster-brothers the dab-chick and water-rat.

Pagan Papers was Grahame's first attempt to realise his pastoral dream in print. His Pan is essentially himself, the lone wanderer by the Thames who talks to the animals and communes with the landscape. In his memoirs Graham Robertson, who used to go walking with Grahame, recalled 'he had a marvellous gift of silence. . . . He would slowly become part of the landscape and a word from him would come as unexpectedly as a sudden remark from an oak or a beech.'[4] And a visitor to Cookham in Grahame's retirement was shown the home of a water rat with the explanation, 'He's quite a friend of mine. Evidently he's gone on some excursion. I shall hear about it one day.'

Pagan Papers is a holiday romance: stockbrokers disappear

from their desks to escape into the countryside or become tramps, a cashier spends his vacation as a turnpike man, and a gentle Pan lures them on by piping out songs of the rural myth. It was lapped up by Londoners who, like Grahame, had no intention of leaving the City but liked to play at being country gentlemen. It was week-end Pantheism, love of nature as an escape, as an anchor against changing ways and a disappearing rural tradition, and as a symbol of spiritual possibility in an increasingly secular age. Grahame's Pan, like Barrie's, is also the free spirit who never grows up.

Though Grahame was loosely chained to the Bank, the 1890s were his freest and happiest years. He was single, popular and rich; he was becoming a respected writer; his thoughts and time were his own, yet his favourite subject accorded fortunately with the fashions of the age. It was in this heady mood that his two bestsellers about childhood, *The Golden Age* in 1895, and *Dream Days* in 1898, were written. Without them, *The Wind in the Willows* would never have seen the light of day.

'Every reader's autobiography' was how one contemporary reviewer described *The Golden Age*, Grahame's stories about a group of orphaned children living with unsympathetic relatives in a large country house. It was Grahame's own idealised autobiography, recreating not only the circumstances of his own childhood but keeping faith with himself as still a child. 'I feel I should never be surprised to meet myself as I was when a little chap of five, suddenly coming round a corner. The queer thing is, I can remember everything I felt then, the part of my brain I used from four till about seven can never have altered,'[5] he said when he returned to his grandmother's Thames-side village at Cookham.

The Golden Age opens with an essay on 'The Olympians', the uncomprehending, stupid adults who with rules, regulations and officious organisation thwart the freewheeling orphans held reluctantly by their authority. It ends, ten years before *Peter Pan*, with one of the most eloquent pleas against growing up in 1890s literature:

Well! The Olympians are all past and gone. Somehow the sun does not seem to shine so brightly as it used; the trackless meadows of old time have shrunk and dwindled away to a few poor acres. A saddening doubt, a dull suspicion, creeps over me. *Et in Arcadia ego* – I certainly did once inhabit Arcady. Can it be that I also have become an Olympian?

Throughout the book and its successor *Dream Days*, the children play, fight, explore, most of all imagine. They take, for example, a magical pretend-journey through paintings in a storybook. The adults, by contrast, are narrow, blinkered, dull; the only ones exempt from Olympian folly are social mavericks, mostly a series of bachelor solitaries, who alone among adults befriend the children. In a key story 'The Roman Road' a travelling painter helps the children in their search for the golden city. The Romantic/Victorian legacy – children and artists alone are visionaries – is for Grahame preserved intact.

Yet *The Golden Age* and *Dream Days* brought the Romantic myth of childhood into an 1890s context. They were best-sellers because they brought to a peak the new fashionable genre of writing about children, but they were also radically innovative. In their introduction, as a group hero, of a set of children governed by egoism, rivalry, scorn, violence, pride and vulnerability, they recorded children's behaviour with a measure of realism for the first time. Though interrupted by whimsical authorial mutterings about the delights of youth, this was a vital breakthrough in the depiction of children in English literature: no child figures, from Dickens's senti-mental heroes and heroines in the 1840s, through Alice in the 1860s to Little Lord Fauntleroy in the 1880s, had been such vivid, independent and flawed characters, rather than symbols, since children first appeared in fiction. Grahame's effect was enormous in determining the future of children's writing. He had an influence on E. E. Nesbit and her stories about the Bastable children and *The Railway Children*, on Frances Hodgson Burnett, who progressed from the moralistic *Fauntleroy* in 1886 to the psychologically compelling *The*

Secret Garden in 1911, and, via them, on the many family stories which dominated children's writing in the first half of this century.

The Golden Age and *Dream Days* were Grahame's clean version of the 'playboy culture' of the nineties, but they were more than formula-writing: they were Grahame's wrestling with the problem of growing up. The last story of *Dream Days*, written in 1898 and called 'A Departure', reveals this most clearly. It is an account of a group of toys, and it opens cosily: 'In moments of mental depression, nothing is quite so consoling as the honest smell of a painted animal.' But the orphan heroes, outgrowing their toys, overhear an 'Olympian' plot to distribute dolls, jack-in-the-boxes and spinning tops to charity children. Making an agonised selection, they decide to save their favourites by burying them underground during 'Moonlightland and Past-Ten-O'Clock-Land'. They debate, for instance, on Leotard, a cardboard acrobat who swings round in a toy theatre to address a painted audience 'watching the thrilling performance with a stolidity which seemed to mark them out as made in Germany', and eventually he is sacrificed:

> But surely, had Leotard heard and rightly understood all that was going on above him, he must have sent up one feeble, strangled cry, one faint appeal to be rescued from unfamiliar little Annies and retained for an audience certain to appreciate and never unduly critical.

Sentimental, middle-class, safe, the story was written out of Grahame's own passion for toys, which continued through his life. 'His special room . . . was most characteristic', recalled his friend Graham Robertson. 'It looked like a nursery. Books there were certainly, but they were outnumbered by toys. Toys were everywhere – intriguing, fascinating toys which could hardly have been conducive to study.'[6] 'The Departure', a celebration of toys contemporaneous with Tchaikovsky's ballet *The Nutcracker* and Collodi's story *Pinocchio*, is an achingly nostalgic and lovingly detailed account of the pleasures of childhood. The intensity lies in the renunciation. In this final story Grahame is trying to bury his own childhood and his sense of himself as a child. A year after it was written, he abandoned his bachelor life, married, and had a son.

'Love is all very well in its way, but friendship is much higher', says the Water Rat in Oscar Wilde's story 'The Devoted Friend'. It was the *fin de siècle* creed, and one which Grahame adopted for his own bachelor Water Rat in *The Wind in the Willows*. One motive for writing the book, he said, was 'by simply using the animal to get away . . . from weary sex-problems'. In the decade between *Dream Days*, when the toys are buried and the children are left on the verge of growing up, and *The Wind in the Willows*, Grahame had his own disastrous attempt at growing up through marriage and parenthood. During these ten years he wrote nothing; the second book marks his return, in imagination at least, to the earlier ideal of the country bachelor life. In it all the pent-up longings and desires to rush from the responsibilities and constrictions of adult life find a liberating creative expression.

In temperament, Grahame was like his predecessors, Lear, Carroll, Hans Christian Andersen – a gentle, eccentric bachelor with romantic fantasies but a horror of close relationships. It was ironically the romantic sentiment of *The Golden Age* that drew him to the woman he was to marry. Elspeth Thomson, born a few years after Grahame in 1862 into a middle-class Edinburgh family much like his own, was by the 1890s a bluestocking hostess keeping house for her stepfather in Kensington. As a child, she had been a kind of precocious 'Alice' who made friends with Tennyson and Mark Twain; in her thirties she was always on the look-out for literary men to join her circle. She had published pseudonymously a coy novel about a working-class girl, *Amelia Jane's Ambition*, but her real passion was for the whimsical and fey writings of the 1890s, and she fell in love first with *The Golden Age* and then with its author, whom she met in 1897. The following year Grahame became Secretary of the Bank and a contemporary photograph shows how eligible he must have been. He looks courteous, honourable, successful and solid, yet still vulnerable; the eyes suggest a lost, uncertain child.

By 1899 the strong-minded spinster and her naive prey, both almost forty, were exchanging baby-talk letters which belonged to the world of sentimental fantasy but led inexorably to marriage. Like Barrie, Grahame succumbed to matrimony when he was recuperating from an illness. While he was resting in Fowey with his Cornwall friends, Elspeth sent him presents, baby-letters, implications that their names were somehow linked. Grahame, ill and cloudy-headed, returned toy-obsessed letters about bachelor exploits:

> We found a drore full of toys wot wound up, and we ad a great race tween a fish, a snaik, a beetle wot flapped is wings, & a rabbit.

'By the way,' he asked Elspeth, 'oos lookin arter my drorful o dolls at ome?'[7] She replied suggesting a fairy-tale Love-Post; Grahame, now concerned for his honour, wrote that he worried about her relentless Kensington social life but that he must talk to her stepfather 'cos I think it wos time you was "brort to your bearins" '.[8] The announcement of the engagement astonished all who knew either of them, and there is a story that Grahame's sister, reading it in *The Morning Post*, demanded to know if it was true and was answered by a sadly low-key Kenneth, 'I suppose so, I suppose so.'

Grahame had been single for forty years and his horror of deep involvement now took over. He wrote in a panic two weeks before the wedding:

> Darlin, ow'd you like ter go on livin at Ons: Sq: & cum away wif me fer week-ends? Then . . . you needn't rite no notes & it wood be so nice & immoril & yet nobody coodnt find no forlt not even arnts.[9]

But Elspeth was not to be put off. She arrived in Cornwall with her trousseau, rejected her wedding gown at the last minute in favour of a Tess-of-the-d'Urbervilles-style muslin and daisy-chain, and the couple were married while a hurdy-gurdy man ground his organ outside the church.

Both were quite inexperienced, and their letters to other people at this time make clear the huge anxiety about sex which they concealed from each other through baby talk. 'My beastly virtue has been my enemy through life, but once married I will try & be frankly depraved, and then all will go well', Grahame told a friend.[10] But all did not. Three days into the honeymoon at St Ives the Grahames returned to the fishing village of Fowey, Grahame resumed 'messing about in boats' with his Cornwall bachelors, and Elspeth, whom none of his friends could tolerate, was left ashore, a 'martyr to the tides', to write desperately for advice to Mrs Thomas Hardy. The reply, from a woman locked in arid marriage to another romantic but remote writer, was pessimistic:

> I can scarcely think that love proper, and enduring, is in the nature of men. . . . There is ever a desire to give but little in return for our devotion, and affection – theirs being akin to children's, a sort of easy affectionate-ness. . . . Keeping separate a good deal is a wise plan in crises – and being both free – and expecting little . . . it is really a pity to have any ideals in the first place.[11]

Elspeth, immature, frightened, a fantasist whose fairy-tale hopes of marriage built up over thirty-seven years of spinster-hood had been shattered in weeks, now turned sour. As Grahame tried to retreat to easy male companionship, she, back in London, threw herself into a round of entertaining which he hated. The birth in 1900 of their only child, Alastair, might have drawn them closer, but here came the next, crucial and far-reaching, disappointment of Grahame's life. Alastair was born, not only premature and sickly, but with a congenital cataract in his right eye, which was completely blind, and a severe squint in his left. It would not have prevented a happy family life had the Grahames accepted the child's disability, but again here was a crisis too grave to face. Instead, for each of his parents Alastair was doomed, even before he was born, to become the focus of their burnt-out hopes and failed aspira-tions. Grahame wanted for him the dazzling education and success at Oxford that he had been denied. Elspeth, at thirty-eight an obsessive older mother, spoilt her son horribly, dressed him in outrageous clothes and chattered whimsical fantasies at him. Worse, she ignored his disabilities and pumped him with ideas that he was a genius. 'Mouse', as he was called, developed a manic, angry temperament that veered between obstinate arrogance and a miserable awareness of his inability to come up to scratch. By the time he was four, he was uncontrollable, and so was his mother; Elspeth, neurotic about her child, crushed by her marriage, often spent all day stretched out on her sofa, sipping hot water, unwilling to move or go out.

It was at this time that Grahame began telling Alastair bedtime stories to calm him down. 'He had a bad crying fit on the night of his birthday, and I had to tell him stories about moles, giraffes & water-rats (he selected these as his subjects) till after 12', Grahame wrote to a friend in May 1904.[12] The same month was recorded the famous reply by the Grahames' maid when asked by Elspeth why Kenneth was late for dinner: 'He's with Master Mouse, Madam, he's telling him some ditty or other about a Toad.' By 1905 the cast list was complete. A guest arriving to see Kenneth was sent upstairs to the nursery, where she eavesdropped outside the door and then tried to recall the story: 'I know there was a Badger in it, a Mole, a Toad and a Water-rat, and the places they lived in and were surrounded by.'[13]

In this early, oral version of *The Wind in the Willows* the undisputed hero was the Toad, and it was understood, as a joke between father and son, that this naughty, unruly character was based on Alastair himself. Alastair was becoming more difficult. In Kensington Gardens where he walked with his governess at the same time as Barrie's Llewelyn Davies boys, the keeper made an official complaint about his relentless kicking and slapping of other children. 'Mouse' also kicked down the bathroom door to get at Grahame while he was in the bath, and had an ominous, provocative habit of lying down prostrate in the middle of the road when he heard motor cars approaching. As Grahame found it harder to relate to him, the

'As they neared the door it was flung open, and Mr Toad, arrayed
in goggles, cap, gaiters, and enormous overcoat, came swaggering
down the steps.' Toad's character was based on Grahame's unruly
son Alastair.

bed-time stories became the vital link between them. But
Grahame was also retreating back to the world of his own
childhood, and in 1906 he took a decision which brought back
the old idyll of solitary riverside wanderings: he moved his
family from Kensington to a home in Cookham Dene, the
village of his youth and the heart of the Thames backwaters
where as a child he had watched the animals who were now at
the centre of his son's stories.

In 1907, when the Grahames wanted to send their problem
child on a summer holiday with his governess, Alastair's
objection was that he would miss out on the stories. Thus it was
that he was promised a series of letters continuing the
'adventures of Mr Toad' and the first instalments of *The Wind
in the Willows* were written down.

Grahame, locked into marriage, the Bank and anxious
parenthood, had published nothing for ten years and the 1907
letters to Alastair provide a wonderful record of a reawakening
creativity. They began as short episodes immersed in birthday
greetings and news 'To my darling Mouse from your loving
Daddy', intended to amuse the child. But midway Alastair
demanded to change his name to 'Michael Robinson', 'a much
finer name', and the letters, opening formally 'Dear Robinson'
and ending merely 'To be continued', now cover several sides
and were obviously written more for Grahame himself. By the
end of the summer, about a third of what was to be *The Wind in
the Willows* – mostly the story of the Toad – was finished. It
remained virtually unchanged in book form.

The letters were returned to Elspeth by Alastair's governess,
but they had not been written for publication, and when
Constance Smedley, a journalist representing the American
magazine *Everybody's*, got to hear of them and came to
Cookham to persuade Grahame back into print, he turned her
down flat.

> Mr. Grahame seemed as remote and shadowy as the
> countryside; he was encased in the defensiveness which
> dreads coercion; about him was that peculiar English
> aroma of dogs, ploughed fields and firelit libraries. . . .

> But Mr. Grahame refused all entreaties . . . he hated
> writing; it was physical torture. Why should he undergo
> it?[14]

Nevertheless, telling the stories had unleashed imaginings repressed since Grahame's marriage. Constance Smedley cannily befriended Alastair, together they coaxed Grahame to look again at the letters, and within months he was engrossed in a private world which no longer had anything to do with his son or with the idea of publication. He wrote, in a great rush, for himself. Into the book poured all the disappointments, passions, hopes and fears of the grown man, now nearly fifty, who is at once acknowledging the unalterable state of his compromised life, with fantasy his one escape, and lamenting the changing environment around him which, with railroad, motor car and urbanisation, seemed to take him further from the idealised haven of his childhood. As the chaotic, violent worlds of Lear and Carroll reflect the pent-up anger and frustration of the mid-Victorian authors, so the mellow, resigned tones of *The Wind in the Willows*, its gentle lyricism and its passionate plea for conservatism and the traditions that made Grahame feel safe, come out of the particular circumstances of the middle-aged Secretary of the Bank of England suddenly finding in fantasy the chance to express feelings and thoughts bottled up for years.

The Wind in the Willows was written at once in retreat and in affirmation, from a sense of faith and a sense of fear, and in all these aspects it is a quintessential Edwardian book. Sparked by personal frustration, it is a withdrawal from adult life into a celebration of carefree bachelor companionship. Composed while living with a wife who misunderstood his values, it is a potent affirmation of the pastoral ideal which had sustained Grahame since childhood. And inspired by fear that country ways were being swept away for ever, it maintains an almost religious faith in nature and the power of landsape for its own sake. The result is a heady evocation of the English pastoral dream. Among children's writers, only Edward Lear suggests landscape with such feeling and precision as Grahame.

When Grahame came to commit his characters to print, they acquired a depth beyond their adventuring personae in Alastair's bedtime stories which showed how closely the work stemmed from Grahame's own needs, for each in a sense became Grahame himself. The shy awkward Badger, uneasy in everyday society but the perfect gentleman, is that aspect of Grahame which suffered most from Elspeth's pretentious Kensington soirées. Timid, unworldly Mole, with his instinct for home, his solitary underground burrowing, and his choked-up emotions, suggests the Grahame who fled London and settled, far from the madding crowd, in the heart of his childhood home in Cookham Dene.

> He stopped dead in his tracks, his nose searching hither and thither in its efforts to recapture the fine filament, the telegraphic current, that had so strongly moved him. A moment, and he had caught it again; and with it this time came recollection in fullest flood.
>
> Home! That was what they meant, those caressing appeals, those soft touches wafted through the air, those invisible little hands pulling and tugging, all one way! . . . Poor Mole stood alone in the road, his heart torn asunder, and a big sob gathering, gathering, somewhere low down inside him. . . .

And most of all the Water Rat, part-time poet and dreamer, tempted by fleeting visions of escape to southern shores, but held back by his responsibility towards friends and his everyday life, is Grahame after marriage, the would-be wayfarer who cannot quite 'heed the call' of the Sea Rat:

> . . . the days pass, and never return, and the South still waits for you. Take the Adventure, heed the call, now 'ere the irrevocable moment passes! 'Tis but a banging of the door behind you, a blithesome step forward, and you are out of the old life and into the new!

For the Water Rat, as for Grahame, the 'cure' is his pen, which renders him 'absorbed and deaf to the world; alternately scribbling and sucking the top of his pencil'.

All are free-spirited single boys who never age, and this is Grahame in exultant retreat. The book, he boasted, was 'clean of the clash of sex'; he told President Roosevelt that its 'qualities, if any, are mostly negative – i.e. no problems, no sex, no second meanings – it is only an expression of the simplest joys of life as lived by the simplest beings'. But instead of sex, there are the sensual pleasures that continued to console Grahame. There is communion with the natural world. The gift observed by Grahame's friends, his ability to merge effortlessly with natural surroundings, is communicated to his characters, who exist only within the living detail of landscape precisely delineated. Thus we remember Alice or Peter Pan for what they say or do, but Mole and Toad and Rat are unimaginable without the context of the river bank; and river, wild wood and Toad Hall are characters as vivid as the animals. So exact and evocative was Grahame's description of the river bank that *The Wind in the Willows*, unique among the classic fantasies, was never envisaged with illustrations; when early illustrators tried, the skilful perspective with which Grahame had integrated animal and background eluded them, and not until the 1920s did E. H. Shepard achieve success. ('The Toad was train size, the train was Toad size', Grahame explained, and in the text the Toad diminishes easily in half a line from dashing brigand to 'nasty crawly' amphibian flung into the river.)

It is through minutiae of finely chiselled sensual impressions that Grahame builds up the broad scope of the pastoral drama of the changing seasons. Only Evelyn Waugh in the war-time reminiscences in *Brideshead Revisited* approaches Grahame's technique, for example, of imbuing food with a precisely evoked nostalgia for time, place and English tradition:

> . . . a plate piled up with very hot buttered toast, cut thick, very brown on both sides, with the butter running

Messing about in boats.

through the holes in it in great golden drops, like honey
from the honeycomb. The smell of that buttered toast
simply talked to Toad, and with no uncertain voice; talked
of warm kitchens, of breakfasts on bright frosty mornings,
of cosy parlour firesides on winter evenings, when one's
ramble was over and slippered feet were propped on the
fender.

It works again with the temptations of the south – 'a sausage out
of which the garlic sang, some cheese which lay down and
cried, and a long-necked straw-covered flask containing bottled
sunshine shed and garnered on far Southern slopes' – or with
the sense of warmth and cold, romance and loneliness, which
evoke universal pleasures and hardships in Rat and Mole's
pre-Christmas trudge through a snow-bound village:

> But it was from one little window, with its blind drawn
> down, a mere blank transparency on the night, that the
> sense of home and the little curtained world within walls
> . . . most pulsated. Close against the white blind hung a
> bird-cage, clearly silhouetted, every wire, perch, and
> appurtenance distinct and recognisable, even to yester-
> day's dull-edged lump of sugar. . . . Then a gust of bitter
> wind took them in the back of the neck, a small sting of
> frozen sleet on the skin woke them as from a dream, and
> they knew their toes to be cold and their legs tired, and
> their own home distant a weary way.

Home, longing, the outsider pining to get in, echo through *The
Wind in the Willows* as they do in many Edwardian children's
books. *Peter Pan*, Hodgson Burnett's *A Little Princess*
(1905), E. E. Nesbit's *The Railway Children* (1906) are all
concerned with getting back to lost homes. Grahame's ability,
however, was to distil into this sense of snug sweetness the
timeless human conflicts which for him had come to a head
with marriage – freedom versus responsibility, adventure
versus hominess; adaptation to change versus panic at the
disappearing ways – and to find some resolution to them, in an
all-embracing faith in Nature. Where *The Golden Age* and
Dream Days, Grahame's bestsellers from the 1890s, are calm,
moderate, self-conscious accounts of children's friendships

and quarrels, their mood ruffled only by the advance of Time, which will destroy childhood, *The Wind in the Willows* is full of contrasts and tensions, its very structure setting up conflict as the Toad chapters, announcing the pleasures of the Open Road, alternate with the River Bank sections, rhapsodising over the comforts of home. The two 'mystical' chapters, 'Wayfarers All' and 'The Piper at the Gates of Dawn', stand outside this pattern and played no part in the original stories told to Alastair; yet here, in a white heat of imagination, Grahame tries to find a spiritual core to both his sets of longings. So the wayfaring Sea Rat, an Ancient Mariner alighted on the river bank, 'his eye lit with a brightness that seemed caught from some far-away beacon', offers escape to the South in semi-Messianic terms ('heed the call!'), while the piper Pan is a pagan version of the 'Friend and Helper' of Victorian Christianity, protecting the river bank, ensuring the lost animal gets safely home, a creature of home comfort and of rural myth:

> . . . while Nature, flushed with fullness of incredible colour, seemed to hold her breath for the event, he looked in the very eyes of the Friend and Helper; saw the backward sweep of the curved horns . . . the rippling muscles on the arm that lay across the broad chest, the long supple hand still holding the pan-pipes. . . . All this he saw, for one moment breathless and intense . . . and still, as he looked, he lived; and still, as he lived, he wondered.
> 'Rat!' he found breath to whisper, shaking. 'Are you afraid?'
> 'Afraid?' murmured the Rat, his eyes shining with unutterable love. 'Afraid! Of *Him*? O, never, never! And yet – and yet – O, Mole, I am afraid!'
> Then the two animals, crouching to the earth, bowed their heads and did worship.

Today, this is the section most readers skip as unpalatably sentimental, but for Grahame, who placed it deliberately at the centre of the book, it embodied the vision which inspired his thinking. The highly charged rhetoric, the Christian imagery and tone transferred to a secular context, the hazy sense of half-understanding, of magic and mystery, the worship of nature which is implicated in the spiritual experience, all are typical ingredients of Edwardian writing. In a society where Christian observance was no longer *de rigueur*, where theological passions and idealisms were spent, the old religious forms and images were called in to service new spiritual experiments. Any mystic experience – William James's *Varieties of Religious Experience* (1902) suggested all were equally valid – aroused interest, and paganism became the most popular of the secular adaptations. Brooke's enthusiasm for fellowship and naturism, Moore's pagan baptism in *The Lake* (1905), Forster's 'only connect', the 'chalice of youth' offered at the lake in *A Room with A View* (1908): all these echo Grahame's pagan sentiments. Paganism explains, too, the craze for animal characters in adult stories. *The Wind in the Willows* is only one example; Richard Jeffries' accounts of riverbank life, *Bevis* and *Wood Magic*, and Wilde's story 'The Devoted Friend' included talking rodents in the 1890s. And so pervasive was the mood that children's books such as *The Wind in the Willows*, *Peter Pan* and *The Secret Garden* rose to the same crescendoes of mystical exultation as adult fiction: 'I'm youth, I'm joy. I'm the little bird that has broken out of the egg' cries Peter Pan. In *The Secret Garden*, the cripple Colin, cured by the great outdoors, echoes him with 'I am going to live for ever and ever and ever!', while his father Mr Craven, whose awakening takes place in the 'magic' natural garden, recalls the spirit of Rat and Mole's discovery of Pan: 'What is it?' he said, almost in a whisper. . . . 'I almost feel as if – I were alive!'

The pagan obsession, evident in literature since the Romantics, intensified as the country traditions it celebrated were felt to be threatened. This lends an elegiac quality to nineteenth and early twentieth-century writing about rural life, best known in the work of Thomas Hardy and Kenneth Grahame. Both were engaged by the rural myth – Hardy's characters are as set into their Wessex landscape as Grahame's are into the Thames-side idyll – and both pit the majesty and timelessness of rural traditions against a 'modernist' enemy who would destroy them. In *The Wind in the Willows*, the motor car is the humorous expression of Grahame's terror of change, industrialisation and modern life.

> . . . the peaceful scene was changed. . . . The 'poop-poop' rang with a brazen shout in their ears, they had a moment's glimpse of an interior of glittering plate-glass and rich morocco, and the magnificent motor-car, immense, breath-snatching, passionate . . . possessed all earth and air . . . flung an enveloping cloud of dust that blinded and enwrapped them utterly. . . .

Toad, the motor car maniac, is the Edwardian upper-class yobbo whose uncouth ways threaten to bring into disrepute and danger the very class whose role is to preserve the old order:

> 'You knew it must come to this sooner or later, Toad,' the Badger explained severely. 'You've disregarded all the warnings we've given you, you've gone on squandering the money your father left you, and you're getting us animals a bad name in the district by your furious driving and your smashes and your rows with the police. . . .'

As the one animal who heeds the call of the open road, Toad endangers the social order and is alone the character whom Grahame knows he can never be, and whose come-uppance the conservative, middle-class author would never have risked. When Toad finds himself penniless, his is the classic nightmare of Victorian and Edwardian loss of respectability:

> To his horror he recollected that he had left both coat and waistcoat behind him in his cell, and with them his pocket-book, money, keys, watch, matches, pencil-case – all that makes life worth living, all that distinguishes the many-pocketed animal, the lord of creation, from the inferior one-pocketed or no-pocketed productions. . . .

For Grahame, abandoned as a child, unable to afford Oxford, solitary by nature, the Bank of England was a haven which ensured financial security and superficial conformity. 'I must not wish you luck in your nefarious designs on our savings, our cellars and our garden-plots', he wrote to his liberal friend Quiller-Couch before an election. His conservatism and fear of the mob was exacerbated in 1903 when he was shot at in the Bank of England by a lunatic-anarchist who broke into the building – an incident which possibly inspired the ransacking of Toad Hall by the proletarian stoats and weasels.

On the other hand, all the characters in *The Wind in the Willows* are in some sense social mavericks, loners with their individual worldviews and dreams, and here Grahame belongs to the fantasy tradition stretching from Lear to Milne and beyond. But he is not an anarchist in Lear or Carroll's mould, and social propriety, the importance of fitting in, is imbedded in *The Wind in the Willows*. Grahame once recorded a nightmare in which job and home were surreally snatched from him: it was, fundamentally, the nightmare of not fitting in. He dreamt 'that the house was broken into by burglars, and he wanted to get up and go down and catch them, but he could not move hand or foot.'

> He heard them ransacking his pantry, stealing his cold chicken and things, and plundering his wine-cellar. . . . Then he dreamt that he was at one of the great City Banquets that he used to go to . . . he thought of a most excellent speech. . . . And he tried to make it, but they held him down in his chair and wouldn't let him. And then he dreamt that the Chairman actually proposed his own health – the health of Mr Grahame! and he got up to reply, and he couldn't think of anything to say! And he stood there, for hours and hours it seemed, in a dead silence, the glittering eyes of the guests – there were hundreds and hundreds of guests – all fixed on him. . . . Till at last the Chairman rose, and said 'He can't think of anything to say! *Turn him out!*'[15]

The two sides of Grahame – the conventional banker and the reclusive writer – both play their part in *The Wind in the Willows*, and it is this aspect that led C. S. Lewis to observe, 'the child who has once met Mr Badger has got ever afterwards, in its bones, a knowledge of humanity and English history which it certainly couldn't get from any abstraction'. This is the great pull of the book: from Grahame's innermost fears and aspirations come characters which a century on remain emblematic types of the English myth of class and countryside, as well as imaginative symbols of timeless hopes and anxieties.

The Wind in the Willows had a hard ride into print. At first, it failed to find a publisher at all: 'I tried it with magazine editors all over England and America. They thought it too fantastic and wouldn't have it', wrote Grahame's agent Curtis Brown.[16] Eventually, an old fan, Theodore Roosevelt, who had seen the manuscript, persuaded Scribners to take it on in America. In England, Methuen risked it, though without the confidence to pay an advance, and with such pessimism about any sales that Curtis Brown got them to agree 'excellent rising royalties, just in case the book should fulfil my dreams'. No one could settle on a title. Grahame wanted 'Mr Mole and his Mates'; Methuen advertised it as 'The Wind in the Reeds', the original title of the Pan chapter, then found this too close to the title of a collection of Yeats's poetry; *The Wind in the Willows* was a last resort. And the critics hated it. 'As a contribution to natural history the work is negligible', said *The Times*, and even sympathetic reviewers were baffled; Arthur Ransome wrote: 'If we judge the book by its aim, it is a failure, like a speech to Hottentots made in Chinese. And yet, for the Chinese, if by any accident there should happen to be one or two of them among the audience, the speech might be quite a success.'[17]

But none of this mattered, for in the six months after publication, from October 1908, the book went into four editions; there were another three by 1912, and when Shepard illustrated the work in 1931, a year before Grahame's death, *The Wind in the Willows* was in its 38th edition. An instant bestseller, its popularity has never waned.

It had little effect, however, on Grahame, who was more reclusive than ever. In 1908, before the book appeared, he retired from the Bank of England, and in 1910 he moved from Cookham, which was getting too modern, to a Tudor farm-house in Blewbury, near Didcot: 'All the houses here are very old. They do not build the horrid little red houses that spring up around Cookham', he wrote. He refused to be drawn back into print, and spent each day on a long solitary tramp across the Berkshire Downs. Elspeth stuck to the sofa and hot water, Alastair was sent to school and exchanged coy letters with his mother in which his father was nicknamed 'Inferiority'. ('My dear Madame, your humble servant is glad to hear that improvements are coming up like bulbs and that Inferiority is doing some work at last', he wrote, aged eleven.) Visitors were rare, their reception eccentric; the son of an American friend of Grahame's wrote of a visit:

> Mr and Mrs Grahame lived in separate parts of the house. My parents were very connubial and the Grahames simply expected their guests to enjoy the same household and sleeping arrangements as they themselves did. . . . At breakfast, after this nocturnal separation of the sexes there was tea and toast and one egg. Mrs Grahame said: The egg is for Kenneth.[18]

Yet, given a chance, the old courtesy surfaced. Roosevelt, lecturing at Oxford, demanded a meeting and found Grahame 'simply charming'. An American professor who made the pilgrimage to Blewbury noted that once out of the house and on the Downs in his knickerbockers and baggy tweed coat, the taciturn writer 'would break into an easy current of cheery conversation'. In a photograph from this time at Blewbury Church Feast, Grahame is a dignified, handsome, meaty figure, his impressive moustache now white, the far-away but intense look in his eyes still there.

The Grahames played no active part in the war, though its privations intensified their isolation. Grahame dreamt of the day when there would be feasts again. Their energy concentrated on Alastair, who entered Rugby in 1914 but lasted just a term. Shy, squinting, half-blind, his imagination nourished on Elspeth's fairy tales and Grahame's river-bankers, he fared badly at Eton too, where the Grahames sent him against the advice of friends who tried tactfully to point out his oddities and problems. 'Scratch us, we are all barbarians but it happens that I prefer curios and they prefer cricket bats', Alastair wrote from Eton. An emotional breakdown forced him to be removed in 1916. But the Grahames stuck to the dream of a normal schoolboy son; the fatal pressure continued, and Alastair entered Christ Church, Oxford, in 1918, his semi-blindness precluding wartime service.

At Oxford, his tutor remembered him sighing, groaning audibly, and permanently wretched. Poor sight made work a struggle; he was agonisingly reserved, though he had more sympathetic companions than at school; he no longer confided in his parents. And still the river bank haunted him: 'Of course I was not surprised at the news, for we were both determined that nothing else should happen, were it only for the Toad's sake!', wrote a friend when he passed Mods. Two months later, days before his twentieth birthday in May 1920, Alastair was found dead on the railway track at Port Meadow. Like the death of another intolerably pressurised Oxford under-graduate, Barrie's protégé Michael Llewelyn Davies, just one year later, it was suicide made to look like an accident. A verdict of accidental death was recorded, but the coroner's report made it clear that Alastair had not been knocked down but had lain across the line some way from a level crossing and waited for a train to run him over.

Grahame had twelve years left to live. Almost at once he closed up the house in Blewbury and he and Elspeth fled to Italy, beginning half a decade of restless wandering which took them all over the Mediterranean. When, in his mid-sixties, Grahame could face returning to settle in England, he chose a riverside home in Pangbourne, and it was here that E. H. Shepard visited him with a project for new illustrations for *The Wind in the Willows*.

> . . . . he said 'I love these little people, be kind to them'. Just that; but sitting forward in his chair, resting upon the arms, his fine handsome head turned aside, looking like some ancient Viking, warming, he told me of the river near by, of the meadows where the Mole broke ground that spring morning, of the banks where Rat had his

house, of the pools where Otter hid, and of Wild Wood way up on the hill above the river. . . .[19]

Although *The Wind in the Willows* was written at Cookham, Shepard's magnificent and sensitive illustrations bear the stamp of this stretch of the Thames; his Toad Hall, for example, is modelled on Mapledurham House near Pang-bourne.

Toad Hall, which E. H. Shepard drew from Mapledurham House near Pangbourne. ' "Toad's rather rich, you know, and this is really one of the nicest houses in these parts." '

At the same time as Shepard's visit, A. A. Milne, who had written Grahame a fan letter in 1918, adapted *The Wind in the Willows* into a children's play, *Toad of Toad Hall*. 'When characters', wrote Milne, 'have been created as solidly as those of Rat and Mole, Toad and Badger, the dramatist has merely to listen and record',[20] but the sentimental, twee and perennially popular play bears as much the mark of Milne as of Grahame. Milne had once demanded a sequel to the book, 'a second wind', but Grahame had declined. The war, Alastair's death, the fast-changing character of Thames villages like his child-hood Cookham, all had come between the older, irrevocably saddened Grahame and the author who in 1908 could still believe in the ideal world of his fantasy. It was Milne, in a different social and cultural climate, who tried, without the sustenance of Grahame's pagan faith, to recapture the pre-war Edwardian summer in the last great children's fantasy. Grahame saw the Pooh books come into print in the 1920s. In 1932, a few weeks after his last visit to London, for the Lewis Carroll centenary celebrations, he died of a cerebral haemor-rhage. He is buried in Holywell cemetery in his favourite city, Oxford.

6

A. A. Milne:
the Fantasy Tamed

So they went off together. But wherever
they go, and whatever happens to them on the
way, in that enchanted place on the top of the
Forest a little boy and his Bear will always be
playing.

A. A. Milne
The House at Pooh Corner

A A. Milne bucks the trend set by every other famous
. writer for children. He comes at the end of a line of
authors, stretching from Andersen and the brothers Grimm
through Lear and Carroll, Barrie and Grahame, Nesbit,
Hodgson Burnett and Beatrix Potter, who in a century
revolutionised children's writing, created a new form of
bestseller, and established the ideal of a children's classic which
still holds today. But where the other great children's writers
had lives sad, unfulfilled or in some way marked by tragedy,
Milne's life until his last years was almost unclouded in its ease,
happiness and worldly success. Where many of the others
invented in fantasy the ideal youth they never knew, Milne had
an idyllic childhood whose mood the Pooh stories recapture.
Where the others were mostly childlike and therefore childless,
telling stories to other people's offspring in wistful attempts to
get close to children, he was a contented husband with a son
whom he adored. And where the others were mavericks,
lonely, eccentric, emotionally unbalanced or odd in appear-
ance, Milne was handsome and clever, well-off and well-liked.

His misfortune was that in a casual moment one holiday, he
wrote a few poems and then stories for children which made
him rich and famous and which became so popular that he was
never allowed to forget them. Eventually they came between
him and everything else he wanted to do, and caused his
estrangement from his beloved son. The Pooh stories sprang
from his own happiness just as Carroll's or Barrie's fantasies
grew out of their disappointments. In a horrible way, they then
destroyed the very idyll they celebrated.

Milne and his son were the last victims of the literary obsession with childhood, and their story is tied to the development of British cultural life in the first part of this century. It is entirely appropriate that by the 1920s, when Pooh was created, the great new fantasy writer was neither an eccentric, non-literary outsider like Lear or Carroll nor an unusual literary personality like Barrie or Grahame, but a conventional member of the English establishment whose work and life reflected the widespread desire for lightheadedness, escape and post-war fun. For by the time Milne was writing after the First World War, the cult of the child, which had been a matter of passionate belief for the Victorians and of earnest idealism for the Edwardians, had turned into pure escapist whimsy: mawkishness based not on a Wordsworthian faith in the purity of children and nature but on a desperation to be flippant, unchallenged, intellectually and emotionally cosy. The 1920s saw the last twinkle of the romance of childlike innocence become decadent before it flickered out altogether in the depressed 1930s. Milne represents the fantasy tamed. Instead of Grahame's or Potter's real animals, his models are toys bought at Harrods; instead of Barrie's and Grahame's Pan, wild god of nature and spiritual core of the Edwardian classics of childhood, his god-like figure is a six-year-old who has just started school and cannot spell.

It is tempting to dismiss Pooh as the epitome of romantic innocence turned degenerate. And yet, Milne created in the Hundred Acre Wood a fantasy world as strong and definitive as Wonderland or Neverland, with characters more popular than any in children's literature. A century after Wordsworth, his was an original vision of the golden age of childhood that had obsessed generations of writers. No one who did not believe at some level in the idyll could have written it. But Pooh's forest is also shot through with irony. Milne knows the bathos, the unreality, of his stuffed toys as well as their nostalgic power. Twenty years on, he could not have said, as Grahame did, that he loved his characters, or like Barrie, that their meaning for his own life was clear. His fantasy survives its sweetness and sentimentality just because he does not wholly believe it, because he suffuses it with self-mockery which even very young readers enjoy.

That mockery is the death-knell of the children's fantasy. Milne wrote, half-jokingly, within the trend for cosy escapism, and when that fashion passed, no one else could even pretend to so powerful a vision of childhood. His are the last characters to join the great creatures of fantasy – morose Eeyore, timid Piglet – to whom we still turn as human types. His catchphrases such as 'time for a little something' are the last in a fantasy to enter everyday language as naturally as Carroll's 'jam tomorrow and jam yesterday – but never jam today' or Grahame's 'messing about in boats'. No children's book since has approached *Pooh*'s mythic status. The story of Milne, his writing and his cultural background, shows why Pooh marked the end of the fantasy tradition.

Alan Milne was born in Hampstead in 1882 and from the start was steeped not only in his own happy family but in the idea of childhood as a glorious and important time. His father was headmaster of a small public school whose alumni included Lord Northcliffe and, among the masters, H. G. Wells. J. V. Milne ran the school with benevolence and enlightenment like an extended family; at prizegiving boys received their books from the headmaster's toddler sons, perched on a table, and no pupil ever recalled the cane being used. Learning was esteemed but discipline relaxed – in his autobiography Milne tells of bowling hoops down to Kilburn and back with his brother before breakfast – and the boys were mothered by Milne's own mother. Forty years on, this child-centred world, brimming with home comforts and affection, where each boy was treated as an individual, where games and friendship merged into scholarship, was recreated as the Hundred Acre Wood of Winnie-the-Pooh and filled with toys who behaved like children.

Alan was his parents' third, last and favourite child, and inherited much of the luck that by tradition goes to the fairy-tale third son: cherubic good looks, charm, a quick brain. He is the star of a photograph from 1886, taken with his older brothers, where all three boys are dressed in Little Lord Fauntleroy suits and collars, hair curling to their shoulders like the bestseller-hero of that year; they sit in a cluster round their schoolmaster-father, who looks every inch the loving, proud Victorian paterfamilias. Alan adored him and his school, begged to go early to lessons and soon outstripped his older brothers. He won a scholarship to Westminster, where he was less indulged and grew lazy, but he followed it with an award to Trinity College, Cambridge. Half a century later he remembered Westminster happily enough to leave it a sizeable portion of his estate.

Milne went up to Cambridge in 1900 as a mathematician with literary ambitions, and his life during the next decade much resembled that of Grahame and Barrie in the 1890s. The old Queen died while he was at Trinity, and the radicalism and high seriousness of Bloomsbury-to-be was already in the air – Lytton Strachey, Leonard Woolf and Clive Bell were all Trinity contemporaries – but Milne took a more traditional path. He showed a talent for light verse, edited the undergraduate journal *Granta*, then a stepping-stone to *Punch*, and left Cambridge with a third-class degree. His fondest memory of his college days, he wrote in a poem, was of salmon mayonnaise and *crème brûlée*.

Photographs of Milne as a young man show a larger but otherwise unchanged version of the cherubic Little Lord Fauntleroy infant. He is blond with bright blue eyes – his wife and son called him Blue; a shining smile and unclouded expression suggest confidence, security, no tormented depths. Some of his childlike charm recalls Barrie: 'I had no beard; I was twenty and very young for that', he remembered of himself at Cambridge. He would joke about his unsophisticated tastes, such as a preference for rice pudding over beer or whisky; later he stuck to acid drops bought in a paper bag rather than his wife's Charbonnel et Walker chocolates. Throughout life he shared Grahame's passion for childlike home comforts, handing them on to Pooh, with his consoling honey pots and jars of condensed milk. His literary idols also pointed to a continuing affinity with childhood pleasures. 'Have you seen *Peter Pan*? It's too wonderful to live', runs a letter to H. G. Wells in 1905, when Milne was twenty-three. *The Wind in the Willows*, published in 1908, became an obsession with him, and he used to judge people by whether or not they liked it. Already, in the 1900s, his life began to overlap with Grahame's and Barrie's. He spent weekends at house parties by the Thames near Cookham, minutes from Grahame's home, at the country retreat of *Punch* editor and socialite R. C. Lehmann, and he identified and loved precisely the stretch of the river which inspired Grahame in the book. He became friends with Barrie, with whom he shared a passion for games, and joined Barrie's cricket club, the Allahakbarries. Literary London opened up to him.

Yet where Barrie and Grahame were tied to an ideal of childhood which prevented adjustment to later experience, Milne's childlike pleasures sat easily in a life whose keynote was stylish trivia; Milne grew simply from happy child into a charming young man excelling in the adult playground of pre-war London. He joined the staff of *Punch* in 1906, and made his mark with two series, 'Bachelor Days' and 'The Rabbits', about a set of fast-talking hedonists who quip at each other across the croquet lawn and play eccentric games like balancing glasses of water on their heads. 'No one can compare with Mr Milne for being silly, wittily, neatly and gracefully', wrote the *Manchester Guardian* when the Rabbits' antics were collected in *The Day's Play* in 1910. The Rabbits became something of an Edwardian cult; over-grown children, successors to Grahame's 1890s *Dream Days* family and contemporaries of Peter Pan, they fix the playful mood of the decade and anticipate on the one hand Pooh and on the other the bright young things of *Vile Bodies*, Evelyn Waugh's satire on a post-war society which still refused maturity.

In 1930, Waugh was waspish about the insouciance of this society; the brittle/naive quality of *Vile Bodies* especially recalls the Rabbits. Like his characters, Milne lived on the surface so as to remain unknowable and invulnerable. 'My father's heart remained buttoned up all through his life', wrote his son Christopher.[1] Milne had no close friends except his brother Ken, and when he married in 1913, he chose a wife whom, he said, uncannily resembled a Rabbit heroine. Dorothy de Selincourt, who changed her name to Daphne as a married woman, was cool, confident, striking and snobbish. She quoted chunks of Rabbit-talk by heart from *Punch* when she first met Milne, and she loved his jokes. They became friends in the sort of independent, equal way which would have been socially impossible a generation earlier, and one winter joined by chance the same ski-ing party in Switzerland. Milne 'proposed to her at eleven o'clock one morning in a snowstorm'. In marriage they stayed friendly rather than passionate. Daphne, according to friends, had little time for sex; there were separate bedrooms from the start. For Milne it was perfect. Daphne was witty, elegant, devoted, a stylish home-maker, but she also had a self-sufficient, unyielding quality which kept emotion at bay. Milne, whose temperament could have made him a bachelor or an unengaged husband in the mould of the other fantasy writers, found in Daphne support and domestic contentment without any demand for intimacy or intensity. It was a long, contented marriage such as none of the Victorian and Edwardian fantasy writers achieved.

War at first hardly seemed to penetrate Milne's world. In *Punch* of 12 August 1914, a week after England had declared war on Germany, a Rabbit heroine says 'I was just thinking that life was very wonderful. But it's a *silly* thing to say.' Milne had been a pacifist, but he enlisted in 1915 – not for him the radical route of Bloomsbury. He had the good fortune to be invalided home from the Somme in 1916 with trench fever, and as a signals officer stayed in England for the rest of the war. The Somme confirmed his pacifist beliefs, which influence *Winnie-the-Pooh* and mark it as a post-war book as emphatically as *Peter Pan* is pre-war. But he spent his time off writing light-hearted plays, and after the war his life was as carefree as before.

Success continued to shower down. Milne was helped by Barrie, and in the early 1920s his brand of whimsical Barriesque comedy, such as *Mr Pim Passes By*, made him one of the best-known and best-paid dramatists in England; today few have heard of one of his plays. Then in 1920, his only child Christopher Robin, known as Billy Moon, was born – Daphne was so horrified by childbirth that she vowed never to endure it again – and Milne, enraptured by his son, became unusually involved in his upbringing. He took a country retreat, Cotchford Farmhouse on the edge of Ashdown Forest in Sussex, and lived in a kind of rural family idyll, writing to his brother in 1927:

> We are terribly happy here. I could go on and on doing nothing but watch Daff weed, and she could go on and on weeding. Really the garden is lovely now. . . . I shall leave something beautiful behind anyway. Moon had a tent, two bantams and a rope ladder among his birthday presents. . . .[2]

The model for Pooh's forest was in place, while Milne's closeness to his own son opened up a vision of youthful preoccupations which was closed even to Carroll or Barrie, who were adoring onlookers of other people's families. Milne was a devoted but realistic parent with a penchant for child themes. The way to Pooh, the only one of the fantasies to depict a convincing child world, was set.

In 1922, Milne wrote the sentimental verses 'Vespers', about his son saying his prayers, as a gift for his wife, and in 1923, at a dull house party in Wales, he retired to the summer house to dash off a children's poem he had promised for an anthology. It was the nonsense rhyme 'The Dormouse and the Doctor'; when it was finished Milne hung about the garden looking for an excuse to avoid the other guests. He scribbled out a few more poems, and by the time he fled the holiday, a quarter of *When We Were Very Young* had been written. He then, like Barrie twenty years earlier, took his doubting American publisher to lunch at the Garrick and persuaded him into what seemed a doomed venture. E. H. Shepard, a *Punch* artist of whom Milne had despaired during his days on the magazine, was commissioned as illustrator, and Methuen, who had gambled on *The Wind in the Willows*, risked an edition of 5,000 in November 1924. Six weeks later, over 40,000 copies were in print in England, the American market was flourishing, reviewers were ecstatic, and Milne was a marked man: the bestselling children's author of the decade.

The following Christmas, the *Evening News* pressed him for a children's piece and he adapted a story he had told Christopher Robin about his teddy bear. The first Winnie-the-Pooh episode appeared on Christmas Eve 1925 under a front-page headline and was broadcast on Christmas Day from all radio stations. *Winnie-the-Pooh*, with more stories, was published in 1926, its successor *The House at Pooh Corner* in 1928, and another volume of poems, *Now We Are Six*, in 1927. All were instant bestsellers and have been ever since.

When Milne wrote the Pooh books he was in his forties, the same age as Grahame and Barrie when they wrote their fantasies, and like them he lost himself in an alternative, Utopian reality. But while by middle age their lives were fixed in loneliness and frustration, Milne was successful, satisfied, happily married. They poured their dreams and disappointments into a wish-fulfilment version of a childhood Paradise, but Pooh reflects Milne's own contentment – an easy life, the lightheartedness which had marked him since Cambridge, memories of a good childhood, pleasure in his son. Peter Pan and Rat, Mole, Badger, tell of their creators' own damaged psyches, but Pooh and the toys are in no sense based on Milne – he had no need to re-invent himself in a child setting. Rather, they reflect simply his son's life. Christopher Robin, who became the best-known child in England, gives his name to the hero. Winnie-the-Pooh is called after his bear, who acquired part of his name in honour of a Canadian grizzly from Winnipeg whom the child had seen at London Zoo. Other characters were also based on his toys. Eeyore was a Christmas present in 1921, Piglet a gift from a Chelsea neighbour, Kanga came from Harrods. Milne claimed he barely had to create these characters, that merely looking at his son's stuffed donkey with the drooping head or at Pooh or Piglet – whose 'likeness' he insisted Shepard capture by sketching them from 'life' in the nursery – told all about their personalities.

Halfway Down.

The Pooh books, with their backcloth of nannies and nurseries, owe much to Barrie's Edwardian world; even the title of the first, *When We Were Very Young*, suggests parental nostalgia, and this powerful nostalgic quality already in the 1920s was part of their appeal. Writing for a post-war generation looking back to a golden age, Milne modelled his Arcadia on those of Barrie and Grahame. The similarities with

The Wind in the Willows are strong: bachelor animals living independent lives in an idyllic rural setting; no single hero but instead a group of strongly defined individuals; the Edwardian ethos of male friendship and loyalty, adventure and the great outdoors, the adventure-by-adventure structure of the story. In the poems, the Twinkletoe fairies, the Lake King's daughter floating on a water lily, the Brownies behind the curtain, recall Barrie but also reflect the craze for fairies which was a feature of 1920s escapism. Milne was writing two years after Arthur Conan Doyle, creator of the super-sleuth Sherlock Holmes, published in *Strand* magazine the sensational 'photographs' of the Cottingley fairies, which he was convinced some Yorkshire children had actually seen and photographed, and which experts 'confirmed' as authentic. Other poems, like 'Hoppity' ('Christopher Robin goes/Hoppity hoppity', said to send adult dinner parties hopping round tables in Kensington and Chelsea), or 'Halfway Down', with its arch pictures of Christopher Robin as an updated Little Lord Fauntleroy perched on the staircase, caught the mood of playful distraction then in demand.

Yet Milne's tone is worlds away from Grahame's intense, pastoral reverie or Barrie's dream of never growing up. The Edwardian works are morally earnest; Milne is a 1920s humorist – ironic, cynical/sentimental, an escapist who knows he is escaping. Barrie, in *Peter Pan and Wendy* in 1911, calls children heartless, but he recalls Wordsworth in the ideal of childhood imagination and innocence expressed in the book:

> On these magic shores children at play are for ever beaching their coracles. We too have been there; we can still hear the sound of the surf, though we shall land no more.

Ten years on, the popular children's writer is a realist. Milne wrote of a child's 'natural lack of moral quality, which expresses itself . . . in an egotism entirely ruthless'. His genius was to fix the character of the archetypal child, in the context of a child's vision, and within the limits of children's language, as no one before or since has ever done. Earlier fantasies are as much about adult longings as childhood pleasures, and adult readers return to find new depths in them. The Pooh stories are primarily children's books; they offer adults only the nostalgia of a child's-eye view. Unlike earlier fantasy writers, Milne is a devastatingly accurate child psychologist. The witty conviction with which he presents his child-centred universe has kept young readers hooked for seventy years. But it also marked the end of an idealism which had provided the climate for the fantasy genre to develop. With Milne, the cult of the innocent child was over.

Instead, here is a world of games, songs and rhymes, food and easy affection, which any child can recognise instantly. The dramas of *When We Were Very Young* are entirely childish – stepping between the lines and squares on the pavement, putting on wellington boots, eating up your supper, washing your hands before tea. The best poems, the ones children recite and adults remember, are all humorous revelations about the workings of a child's mind. There is the child's awestruck diffidence combined with the belief that he is the centre of the world in 'Buckingham Palace':

> They're changing guard at Buckingham Palace –
> Christopher Robin went down with Alice.
> > 'Do you think the King knows all about *me*?'
> > 'Sure to, dear, but it's time for tea,'
> > > Says Alice

There is the fear of desertion and the confusion at adult ways, mockingly reversed in 'Disobedience' when a mother strays out of bounds:

> James James
> Morrison Morrison
> Weatherby George Dupree
> Took great
> Care of his Mother,
> Though he was only three.
> James James
> Said to his Mother,
> 'Mother,' he said, said he;
> 'You must never go down to the end of the town,
> if you don't go down with me'.

There is the teddy bear, who muses in the ottoman about a King of France pictured as fat as himself, and assumes this is the first person he meets on falling out of the window into the adult world: a perfect pastiche of a child's ability to refer all things to himself and to mix fantasy and reality:

> Our bear could only look and look:
> The stout man in the picture-book!
> That 'handsome' King – could this be he,
> This man of adiposity? . . .
>
> 'Are you,' he said, 'by any chance
> His Majesty the King of France?'
> The other answered, 'I am that,'
> Bowed stiffly, and removed his hat;
> Then said, 'Excuse me,' with an air,
> 'But is it Mr Edward Bear?'
> And Teddy, bending very low,
> Replied politely, 'Even so!'

After the conversation, the bear is handed in at the door – 'Your bear, I think' – and deflated to toy-size: a perspective shift as clever as Grahame's with Toad, and one which gives a sense of how fleetingly a child can feel himself first grand and then insignificant.

Winnie-the-Pooh extends this child vision into a fully-fledged fantasy world. Like Wonderland and Neverland, it is ruled by a child-god, but Christopher Robin, although he can neither fly nor make his fellow-characters disappear by calling them a pack of cards, is the most omnipotent of all child-heroes, the *deus ex machina* who makes all come right. There is no Hook, no 'Off with his head', no threat to his safe playground of stuffed toys with its child-props of balloons, twigs, spoonfuls of medicine.

The toys are breathtakingly simple figures who mirror typical child characteristics or moods – timid Piglet, bouncy Tigger, sulky Eeyore. The briefest catchphrases pinpoint them – A Bear of Very Little Brain, a Very Small Animal, the pessimistic tail-less donkey with his 'Somebody must have taken it. How Like Them'. Milne's episodic invention,

Shepard's drawings, cosy versions of *Punch* cartoons, sustain them. At the heart is Pooh, self-centred, affectionate, innocent, bewildered by adult life, obsessed with food, so greedy that he eats Eeyore's birthday present on his way to deliver it – yet loveable in all his stupidity and selfishness. He is an image of every child:

> 'Oh Bear!' said Christopher Robin. 'How I do love you!'
> 'So do I,' said Pooh.

Milne uses the simplest language of any children's author, but he is also the greatest nonsense writer since Carroll and Lear. Language and rhythm; the mad repitition of poems like 'The King's Breakfast' and 'Disobedience', whose distorted perspectives come out best, as in Lear's 'The Akond of Swat', when chanted aloud; nursery-rhyme archetypes like Little Bo Beep, on which Milne elaborates as Carroll had done; nonsense rhymes, chosen as in Lear and Carroll for sound before meaning – dormouse/e-nor-mouse, foxes and sockses, shopses and copses and wopses: all have a timeless appeal for children. But this is also nonsense tamed, domesticated: the teddy bear sleeping in the ottoman, tin soldiers feeding on cream buns, Nurse and Percy in his slippers. Milne retains just a hint of the anarchy of mid-Victorian nonsense – the bears who lurk in wait in 'Lines and Squares', the satire on the self-satisfied doctor and the hapless dormouse, the escaping mamma, and of course the oddball types, from Tigger to Eeyore, whom we have come to expect from a children's classic. But where Carroll invented a wild, unrecognisable wonderland, Milne, the realist, paints children as they are, and brings nonsense into the world of everyday: his characters are middle-class household commodities that seem to emerge out of Harrods, the Chelsea nursery, the Sussex garden.

In the stories, Milne pulls the two strands of fantasy – mid-Victorian nonsense and the Edwardian rural idyll – into clever juxtaposition. What draws both adults and children to the books is the ironic, biting tone mixed in with the safe setting.

Like Carroll, Milne was a mathematician by training and his adventures are simplified versions of wonderland nonsense. The search for the Heffalump, tracking the Woozle, are circular, logical tales, which start from one premise and follow it on to absurdity. Stories like that of Eeyore's tail ending up as a bell for Owl's house have the super-logic of nonsense distortion. Others are parodies, such as the spoof on military adventures in the Expotition to the North Pole, ending with a teddy bear sticking a twig in the ground – this would have been inconceivable amid the Edwardian gravity of Barrie, with his boys shrieking 'Rule Britannia' as the pirates drag out the gangplank, and is a giveaway that Milne was writing in the disillusioned, post-First World War years.

Milne's premise, however, is not a topsy-turvy world but the foolishness of his characters. Where Alice has an identity crisis as she tumbles down a rabbit hole and grows or shrinks, the toys are merely too stupid to remember who they are:

> 'What a long time whoever lives here is answering this door.' And he knocked again.
> 'But Pooh,' said Piglet, 'it's your own house!'
> 'Oh!' said Pooh. 'So it is,' he said. 'Well, let's go in.'
>
> 'Hallo, Rabbit, isn't that you?'
> 'No,' said Rabbit, in a different sort of voice this time.
> 'But isn't that Rabbit's voice?'
> 'I don't *think* so,' said Rabbit. 'It isn't *meant* to be.'
>
> 'Christopher Robin, Christopher Robin!' cried Piglet. 'Tell Kanga who I am! She keeps saying I'm Roo. I'm *not* Roo, am I?'

The mocking tone is everywhere: in the jokes about who can and can't spell, in the intellectual deceits of Owl ('Wol') and Christopher Robin; in the snobbish sense of hierarchy with which the animals try to outdo each other and which the young reader is invited to share by detecting their ruses – Piglet's efforts to conceal his cowardice, Pooh's to hide his greed. It is in part a skit on the pretence and hypocrisy of conventional adult society in anarchic fantasy mode. But it is also Arcadia evoked in all its seasons as an English pastoral dream with the

nostalgic longing of Grahame – the toys snugly visiting each
other's eccentric homes and tree houses and burrows, the
sensuality of a jar of honey or a hum in the snow – yet shot
through with a sense of disbelief and unattainability: Milne
constantly draws attention to the absurdity of his own fantasy.

'The more it snows, tiddely pom –'

Yet the nursery-rhyme simplicity of his creations, the comfort
of the Hundred Acre Wood as the enchanted forest of fairy tale,
has given the books an almost folkloric power in British
culture, with characters whom adults continue to quote, types
who have exerted an enormous influence on children's writing
this century.

As if he knew he was the last in a tradition, the only fear in the
Pooh stories is the dread of growing up, moving on, no longer
being able to escape. The second book of poems ends with a
Peter Pan-like wish:

> But now I am Six, I'm as clever as clever.
> So I think I'll be six now for ever and ever.

In the final chapter of *The House at Pooh Corner*, the world of
the toys is about to collapse as Christopher Robin starts school.

His attempt to say goodbye to the toys – his childhood – makes an elegy at once sentimental and genuinely moving:

> Still with his eyes on the world Christopher Robin put out a hand and felt for Pooh's paw.
> 'Pooh', said Christopher Robin earnestly, 'if I – if I'm not quite –' he stopped and tried again – 'Pooh, *whatever* happens, you *will* understand, won't you?'
> 'Understand what?'
> 'Oh, nothing.' He laughed and jumped to his feet. 'Come on!'
> 'Where?' said Pooh.
> 'Anywhere,' said Christopher Robin.
> So they went off together. But wherever they go, and whatever happens to them on the way, in that enchanted place on the top of the Forest a little boy and his Bear will always be playing.

Milne, whether he knew it or not, was bidding farewell to the fantasy genre. He decided that the second volume of poems and the second collection of Pooh stories would be the last – in part to shield Christopher Robin from publicity, in part to avoid the label for himself of children's author. But in both cases, the damage was already done.

In 1929, Milne wrote confidently that 'all I have got from Christopher Robin is a name which he never uses, an introduction to his friends . . . and a gleam which I have tried to follow. However . . . I do not want C. R. Milne ever to wish that his names were Charles Robert.'[3] His worries were well-founded, for Christopher Robin's fame would not die. Pictures of father and son had adorned newspapers and the frontispieces of the books, and in 1933 *Parents Magazine* celebrated Christopher Robin, along with Yehudi Menuhin, Princess Elizabeth, Crown Prince Michael of Romania and child film star Jackie Coogan, as one of the most famous children in the world.

Unlike them, Christopher Robin had neither the background nor the talent to cope with such pressure. As he grew up, the shadow of Pooh was embarrassing and constraining. At

Stowe, his schoolmates mockingly played an old gramophone of 'Vespers', which he had recorded as a child; when eventually they handed it to him, he broke it into hundreds of fragments and scattered them across a field. He was familiarly greeted with lines like 'Hello, Christopher Robin! Still saying your prayers?' He trembled, stammered and was cripplingly shy. Yet he could mould himself only on his father, and could not break away. He was, he wrote later, 'very close indeed to my father, adoring him, admiring him, accepting his ideas'.[4] The two played cricket together, chattered, solved simultaneous equations together on the sofa in the evenings, had childish holidays together in Dorset while Daphne flitted off to the Mediterranean. 'He needed me to escape from being fifty', said Christopher.[5]

For Milne, Christopher was consolation, sustenance, inspiration, the more so as immediately after the Pooh books were finished his personal fortune took a severe downturn. In 1929, the year after *The House at Pooh Corner*, Milne's brother and only close friend, Ken, died. At the same time, Daphne Milne began to drift away from her husband. Intoxicated by the glamour of first nights and the celebrity status Pooh had brought her family, she grew bored when life at the Sussex farmhouse quietened down, and, now rich, she spent long holidays in New York, where there were rumours of an affair with playwright Elmer Rice. Milne, trying to revive his dramatic career in London, also had his name linked with an actress, though there is no evidence of infidelity on either side. But during the 1930s the couple led increasingly separate lives, and Milne was a familiar lone figure at his son's school prize-givings and cricket matches.

Milne's problem in the 1930s, like Christopher's, was that he was ineradicably associated with the Pooh books, and, haunted by their fame, he blamed them for every misfortune:

> It is easier in England to make a reputation than to lose one. I wrote four 'Children's books', containing altogether, I suppose, 70,000 words – the number of words in the average-length novel. Having said goodbye to all that

in 70,000 words, knowing that as far as I was concerned
the mode was outmoded, I gave up writing children's
books. I wanted to escape from them as I had once wanted
to escape from *Punch*; as I have always wanted to escape.
In vain.[6]

In fact, his brand of escapist whimsy, which fitted so well with
the simple themes of childhood in *Winnie-the-Pooh*, was
anyway going out of fashion in the depressed and cynical 1930s.
His adult plays, previously successful, began to flop. *The Ivory
Door*, which he thought one of his best, ran to just twenty
performances in London in 1929, and in 1931 his last play to
reach Broadway came off after fifteen nights. 'When there is
nothing whatever to say, no one knows better than Mr Milne
how to say it', wrote *The Times* of his penultimate play, *Sarah
Simple*. By the end of the decade he was regarded as a spent
force.

Ironically, one more success nailed his colours to the
children's mast when his adaptation of *The Wind in the Willows*
into *Toad of Toad Hall* in 1930 became one of the most popular
children's plays this century. 'In this play one emotion only is
allowed to creep in: nostalgia. And for as long as I knew him
this was the only emotion that he seemed to delight in both
feeling and showing', wrote Christopher Milne of his father.[7]
The Milnes and the Grahames watched the play from the same
box; Grahame made his appreciation felt, wrote Milne, 'almost
as if he were thanking me in his royally courteous manner for
letting him into the play at all, whereas, of course, it was his
play entirely'.[8] As the *Daily Telegraph* critic wrote, 'the Wild
Wood of Mr Grahame's book is quite evidently only a mile or
two away from the Forest in which dwell Mr Milne's own
creations'. Milne was the natural dramatist for Grahame's
story, and he had to look on bitterly as this adaptation became
his only play to be regularly revived.

His pacifist tract, *Peace with Honour*, was well received, but
the title of his autobiography, *It's Too Late Now*, published in
1939, revealed the mood of a man who knew his star was on the
wane. The title also expresses exactly Milne's faith in child-

hood – 'heredity and environment make the child, and the child makes the man, and the man makes the writer; so that it is too late now' – and over half the book is taken up with childhood memories, while Pooh gets just a few pages. The book defines Milne as a writer obsessed with childhood even when he was trying to escape his public image: 'the sun is shining, goodness and mercy are to follow me (it seems) for ever . . . fifty years from now I shall still dream at times that I am walking up Priory Road'. And he transfers to his father the nostalgia he was himself feeling as Christopher Robin grew up:

> Farewell, Papa. . . . 'Well', you will tell yourself, 'it lasted until he was twelve; they grow up and resent our care for them, they form their own ideas, and think ours old-fashioned. It is natural. But oh, to have that little boy again, whom I used to throw up to the sky, his face laughing down into mine. . . .'

This recalls the words of Milne's early mentor Barrie, that 'nothing that happens after we are twelve matters very much'. By the 1930s, this idea was sentimental, out of touch, and so Milne predates it to the 1890s, when he himself was twelve and Barrie was the height of fashion.

His autobiography sold moderately well, though Methuen reduced the advance from £1,000 to £375, but for the rest of his life he continued to watch his adult works fall from fashion while Pooh remained a bestseller. In the Second World War, sales of the Pooh books rose so steeply that Methuen could not get enough paper to keep them in print; even in Sweden translations of *Winnie-the-Pooh* were selling 5,000 copies a year by 1946. In contrast, when Dutton tried to promote Milne's adult titles in America in 1950, over 200,000 were remaindered at below cost. Milne, used since the Edwardian days to a loyal audience, felt marginalised and ignored. His confidence seeped away; the inscription to his nephew in *Birthday Party*, some stories published in 1948, reads:

> Tony, make room for your Uncle –
> somewhere between
> 'Leprechauns by One of Them'

and
– 'What I saw in New South Wales'
– on the shelf that nobody reads –
A. A. Milne

At the same time came the crisis with his son. At eighteen, Christopher won a scholarship to Trinity College, Cambridge, and was promised his father's old rooms, but the Second World War intervened, and for the first time he was able to put some distance between himself, his father, and the childhood portrait which was his public image. Father and son exchanged affectionate, anxious letters during the war, which Milne supported, as in 1914, despite his pacifism. But when Christopher, aged twenty-five, returned home, the strain of forging out an independent life proved as intensely difficult as it had been for Alastair Grahame and for Barrie's Llewelyn Davies boys. Christopher sought, automatically, to follow his father as a writer, then tried several jobs without success. He wrote in his autobiography, *The Enchanted Places*:

> It seemed to me, almost, that my father had got to where he was by climbing upon my infant shoulders, that he had filched from me my good name and had left me with nothing but the empty fame by being his son.[9]

Milne, feeling weak and useless himself, was barely supportive, and father and son failed to communicate:

> Neither of us knew what the other thought. . . . Did he sympathise? Was he resentful? . . . . If I was jealous of him, he was no less jealous of himself. If I wanted to escape from Christopher Robin, so too did he. . . . He at the top of the hill, I at the bottom: we each had our sorrows, our moments of disillusion. We were both of us unwanted.[10]

In 1948, to his parents' distress, Christopher met and married his cousin Lesley de Selincourt, the daughter of Daphne's brother Aubrey, to whom the Milnes had not spoken for twenty-five years. It was the final break between Christopher and his parents. Milne and Daphne grew closer again and lived quietly in Sussex, occasionally entertaining guests, who were served sherry from a Piglet-shaped decanter. In 1952, Milne had a stroke and survived, crippled and miserable, for over three years. Like the other writers of children's fantasies, he ended life childless: Christopher visited just twice and rashly spoke to a journalist once. A hostile article appeared, which Daphne tried to conceal and which Milne never forgave. One of his last letters, to his sister-in-law, reads:

> Did you read Moon's article on me in the *Sunday Dispatch*, when I was supposed to be dying? You'd have been disgusted. Oh well, I lost him years ago, but I still have Daff. Thank God, though I give her a rotten time.[11]

He died in 1956, aged seventy-four. Christopher came to London for the memorial service, which included Pooh's song 'How sweet to be a Cloud', and 'Vespers', recited to an organ accompaniment. Daphne lived another fifteen years, but never saw Christopher Robin again.

For Milne, fame had turned sour with dazzling speed. The Pooh books rested on an appeal to nostalgia, so that in a sense Milne was old-fashioned even when he was the height of fashion, a fact which proved to make Pooh enduringly popular while Milne was soon seen as hopelessly out of date. Here he differed crucially from the other fantasy writers, who all reflect the themes of their times. Carroll's concerns, his highly wrought tone, his vision of chaos, his girl-fixation, were typically mid-Victorian, and strong parallels in language, ideas, images, mark him as a contemporary of, for example, Dickens. The same common ground links Grahame and his vision of Arcadian England to his Edwardian contemporaries, Forster, Saki, Edward Thomas. But Milne was a throwback who had nothing in common with 1920s modernism, and it is incredible that Pooh appeared after *Ulysses* and *The Wasteland*. There was something inauthentic about the Pooh books from the start, which critics very soon picked up.

The 1930s modernists made mincemeat of Milne. Cyril Connolly, reviewing his autobiography, criticised Milne's 'gentlemanly good taste which veils both a shrewd eye on the main chance and perhaps a fear of life', and wrote:

He reminds me of Noel Coward, a pre-war Noel Coward
springing from the same unexpectedly lower middle class
stock, but moving with pre-war acceleration into a smooth
heaven of light verse, cricketing weekends, good society,
whimsical taste and money, money, money.[12]

Parodies also began at once: a pastiche of 'Vespers' – 'Hush,
hush, nobody cares/Christopher Robin's fallen downstairs' –
was followed as early as 1926 by a collection of parodies, *When
We Were Rather Older*, updating the nursery world to the Jazz
Age:

> James James
> Morrison's Mother's
> Had her hair shingled off.
> She's late
> Home for her dinner,
> Being out shooting golf.
> Jim says
> Somebody told her
> That was the modern view,
> And since it's the rage not to be your age, well,
> what can any son do?

Pastiches and variations on Pooh have thrived ever since, most
famously in *Winnie ille Pu* (1960), the Latin translation which
became the first foreign-language bestseller in America, and in
The Pooh Perplex (1963), Frederick Crews's skit on different
schools of literary criticism as a 'student casebook' on Pooh.
Crews's mockery, which as a bonus included much perceptive
criticism of the Pooh books and their times, silenced almost all
work on Milne for decades, and it is still difficult to write a line
about Pooh without hearing Crews's satiric laughter over one's
shoulder. Despite the pastiche, it is of course the very
familiarity and cosiness of Pooh that makes the joke study so
popular and accessible.

> This Sir Edward Bear, Sir Pooh de Bear, is the very image
> of a fat old Tory who passes all his time pampering his
> depraved tastes and reminiscing about his imaginary
> exploits. Substitute port and brandy for condensed milk

and honey, and you will recognise the likeness at once. He is a *flabby* bear, and flabbiness in literature is a thing I detest above all else.

Everyone can laugh at Pooh because everyone knows him, and the very security and middle-class complacency and parochial Englishness of the Pooh world, which has led critics to savage it, are precisely the qualities which continue to endear the books to children and adults more than half a century after they were written.

Epilogue

From
Alice in Wonderland
to *Lolita*

How his heart beat when, among the innocent throng, he espied a demon child, *'enfant charmante et fourbe'*, dim eyes, bright lips, ten years in jail if you only show her you are looking at her. . . . How marvellous were my fancied adventures as I sat on a hard park bench pretending to be immersed in a trembling book. Around the quiet scholar, nymphets played freely. . . . Ah, leave me alone in my pubescent park, in my mossy garden. Let them play around me for ever. Never grow up.

Vladimir Nabokov,
Lolita

A flabby bear; toys bought from Harrods; the cosy Sussex garden: Milne tamed the fantasy, and in so doing heralded its destruction. After Milne, there were no more enchanted places in children's writing, and a tradition which had begun with Carroll's anarchic Wonderland in 1865, continued through Lear's exotic tropical landscapes, Barrie's exciting Neverland island and Grahame's English river-bank Arcadia to the safe rural idyll of Pooh, came to an end. The progression shows how the fantasy worlds of children's books gradually came closer to reality, until eventually the inventiveness of English children's fantasy ran out. Since *The House at Pooh Corner* in 1928, no world evoked in a children's book, with its own language, setting, tone, has entered the collective imagination and remained part of English culture in the way that Wonderland and the Hundred Acre Wood have done. With no children's characters after Milne's can one sum up a human type in a name – Piglet, Eeyore, the Mad Hatter, Toad – and be instantly understood. And no physical world in children's literature since Pooh's has been so immediately vivid, desirable, tangibly different: a self-contained alternative reality which is entirely convincing and satisfying on an imaginative level.

Why did Milne have no successors? At the heart of the matter lies the relationship between a society and its idea of childhood. For children's literature is a cultural barometer, revealing not only a society's idea of the norm of childhood – the portrayal of Alice gives a snapshot of a seven-year-old don's daughter in 1860s Oxford, Barrie's Darling children suggest a typical upper-middle-class Edwardian family – but its self-image and its aspirations. In Victorian and Edwardian England, childhood and the desire for purity were a key part of that self-image, and children's writers therefore expressed ideals and hopes and fears that were shared, albeit unconsciously, by much of their society. The result was the creation of an imaginative world and characters which still have the solid, lasting resonance of myth. Alice in Wonderland remains the archetype of any child or adult encountering the new and extraordinary; Peter Pan the eternal image of any person who does not want to grow up.

Both these characters are emblematic of the security and innocence of their times, both have a confidence untainted by cynicism. There is Alice's unshakeable belief that she can get by with good manners and self-discipline, and her priggish little self-admonishments ('Oh you foolish Alice!'). There is Peter Pan's boy-scout code of honour; his old-world chivalry ('And you a lady; never!', he says when he insists on risking his life to save Wendy); most of all his famous, patriotic 'To die will be an awfully big adventure'. In these aspects, both express the world-views of their creators and of their times. They belong to an age that was more innocent, happy to accept absolute values, less knowing and cynical and relativistic than our own. This intellectual security stands behind Wonderland, Neverland and all the enchanted, Eden-like places of the Victorian and Edwardian imagination.

The First World War shook this confidence irrevocably. England's national self-esteem and position in world affairs were fatally damaged and did not recover. Class hierarchies began to diminish; the thrifty middle classes received another blow with the collapse of the New York Stock Exchange in 1929. Never again could England look at the future with the certainty in the status quo of the Victorians. In 1918 Lytton Strachey satirised the hypocrisy and pomposity of nineteenth-century values in *Eminent Victorians*; in the 1920s Eliot, Huxley, and the radical, cynical, liberalising influence of Bloomsbury were the dominant voices. Carroll's idealisation of a little girl's virtue and good manners, Barrie's romance of honour and British courtesy and a stiff upper lip, belonged to a past age.

It is the post-war revolution in English society and culture that explains the decline of children's fantasies. Milne, a man obsessed with childhood and deeply involved with the childhood of his son, and a writer whose imagination was formed in the 1900s, was an obvious candidate to recreate an Edwardian Arcadia in the 1920s. Nostalgically, he recaptured the physical attributes of the old rural idyll, the escapism, the safe and unthreatened world of Edwardian England, but he could not win back the intellectual confidence, and this is why his books are shot through with mockery of the very idyll he was celebrating. He invented characters who lie and cheat, who are fearful and ignorant, who are self-doubting and confused, in a way that would have been poison to Grahame's upright, public-spirited river-bank animals twenty years earlier.

Winnie-the-Pooh is the only great children's fantasy not shaped by the social or sexual repression of its author. For by the 1920s, attitudes to sex as well as society were changing. The repressive moral climate which had made Carroll and Lear buttoned-up loners and Grahame and Barrie fearful and under-confident husbands were declining. Freud was writing about sexuality and the unconscious as a driving force in human behaviour and art at just the time when Barrie and Grahame were escaping from sex by writing their fantasies. Now Freud and the idea of psychoanalysis were beginning to be known. Sex was more open and widely discussed. There was less reason for adults to escape into a dream of childlike innocence, and at the same time Freud debunked the idea that a child *was* sexually innocent. The child was no longer an appropriate mirror or an ideal for a society: after the First World War, and especially during the depression of the 1930s, England was neither secure, innocent nor optimistic about the future.

A popular image in this decade was Gerard Brockhurst's 1932 print of a naked young girl staring into a mirror with a look that is both self-consciously knowing and confused, sexually aware yet unsure. The picture is called *Adolescence*, and it captures the mood of a number of 1930s novels – Waugh's *Vile Bodies*, Isherwood's *Mr Norris Changes Trains*, Orwell's *Keep the Aspidistra Flying* – which focused on groups of young people who are desperate, cynical, self-conscious, apparently sexually knowing yet anguished beneath the surface. These brittle, fragile, uncertain types were part of a new, post-war generation. Adult novelists no longer focused on children as their Victorian predecessors had done. The romance with childhood was on the way out, and a new infatuation with adolescence was emerging.

Children's fiction of course continued to be written, but nothing matched the energy and imagination and inventiveness of the earlier years. The children's books which have survived from the 1920s and 30s are predictable and plodding – the adventure stories of Arthur Ransome's Swallows and Amazons series and Hugh Lofting's Doctor Doolittle books; the imitation of Beatrix Potter in Alison Uttley's Little Grey Rabbit stories; Mary Poppins, the Peter Pan-like flying nanny who believes that 'everybody's got a Fairyland of their own'. The debt to the rural dream, the Neverland island, the fantasies particularly of Grahame and Barrie, are clear, but none of these works approached their literary quality or their element of myth.

Only Tolkien in *The Hobbit* in 1937, and *The Lord of the Rings*, written in the following years but not published until the 1950s, attempted a work which was original in spirit. He follows the great fantasies in the creation of a tangible, alternative reality, but there is something forced and self-conscious and intellectual about it, like an exercise in updating Anglo-Saxon chronicles (which Tolkien taught at Oxford), and it is perhaps for this reason that it has not entered English culture at the level of myth in the way that Toad and Badger or Pooh and Eeyore have. The world of the Hobbit is not Arcadian – Tolkien, who fought in the First World War, is more concerned with the nature of evil – and it was not created specifically for children; Tolkien's fantasies are enjoyed both by children and by many adults who never read them when young. They mark a transition between the time when fantasy was predominantly a genre of children's writing, and post-war literature, when fantasy became a popular adult genre used by authors as diverse as Angela Carter and Terry Pratchett. In a sense, adult literature has taken fantasy over, and adults now allow themselves the frivolity and poetry of fantastic, unreal places – perhaps because mainstream literature is less fanciful and sentimental than Victorian novels, and so escapist adult fantasies fill a gap.

In the 1920s and 30s, it was only in European children's literature, which emerged in the context of quite different social upheavals and questions of national self-identity, that a powerful and lasting mythical world was created. It has remained in Jean de Brunhoff's courtly, expressive Babar stories, which A. A. Milne persuaded Methuen to publish in English in 1934; in Antoine de Saint-Exupéry's *The Little Prince* – Saint-Exupéry was another children's writer who never really grew up, writing to his mother once that 'I am not sure that I have lived since childhood';[1] in Erich Kästner's *Emil and the Detectives*, where 1920s Berlin becomes a sort of intoxicating urban equivalent of the English secret garden. Unlike their derivative English contemporaries, each of these books is absolutely authentic in its relation to the culture of its times. Kästner, for example, is as close to German expressionist cityscapes as Grahame is to Arcadian paintings of the English countryside.

English children's literature saw something of a renaissance in the 1950s, significantly the modern decade when Britain was at its most optimistic and forward-looking. C. S. Lewis's Narnia chronicles, beginning with *The Lion, the Witch and the Wardrobe* (1950), Michael Bond's *A Bear Called Paddington* (1958), Mary Norton's The Borrowers series (begun 1955) and Philippa Pearce's *Tom's Midnight Garden* (1958) are all modern classics. The influence of the fantasy tradition on each of them is strong.

Paddington Bear is an updated Pooh with a dash of international glamour – he comes from Peru – though the Paddington books are not fantasies but homely stories about a London family where one child happens to be a comically inept bear. *The Borrowers* is an account of a self-contained fantasy world, this time of tiny people who live beneath the floorboards and 'borrow' from the property of those living above. Unlike its Arcadian predecessors, it is an ugly, claustrophobic world whose heroine Arriety cannot wait to leave it; her final escape into everyday adult life is the happy conclusion – the reverse of Christopher Robin's reluctant farewell to the world of his childhood. *The Borrowers* is a post-Freudian text in the way that *Winnie-the-Pooh* is not; beneath the surface of the Borrowers' world is the tortured relationship between Arriety and her Borrower parents, who, amid protestations for her safety, try to keep her a child by preventing her from going 'upstairs' to join the dangerous life of adults.

Fantasy is most powerfully an influence in *Tom's Midnight Garden* and in the Narnia stories. The first is the tale of a long-destroyed secret garden which a 1950s boy discovers by entering the dreamworld of an old lady who was a child in Victorian England; it is a superbly written and psychologically convincing book which depends for its resonance on images culled, consciously or unconsciously, from Hodgson Burnett's classic *The Secret Garden*. Lewis is similarly derivative. In the Narnia books he makes a highly self-conscious attempt to recreate an Arcadian idyll in didactic, Christian terms. Wonderland and Neverland are his models, but his own images and inventions are too unsubtle and intellectually controlled to work as symbol or myth.

It is possible that we do not escape to Narnia or the Borrower kingdom in the same way as we do to Wonderland or the river bank of *The Wind in the Willows* because our imagination has already been caught by the children's fantasies which have become established in the field earlier. English children's books in the 1980s and 90s have continued to take their themes and images and structure from their nineteenth and early twentieth-century precursors, but, perhaps to overcome this, they offer a new twist. The best modern children's writers, Roald Dahl and Janet and Allan Ahlberg, recognising derivativeness as perhaps inevitable, have made a virtue of it by writing books which turn on post-modernist jokes and revisions of established literary texts and conventions. This is not quite as radical as it seems. Many of the poems in *Alice*, such as 'You are old, Father William', are mocking revisions of worthy verses that Victorian children were expected to learn by heart, and Dahl and the Ahlbergs are thus following a well-established anarchic tradition. Their joky, inventive, highly contemporary revisions do, however, place them in the post-modern tradition, and give them a cultural authenticity which most children's literature since the Edwardians has lacked. This sense of being up-to-date probably explains their immense popularity and success as cultural reference points – a success all the greater because late twentieth-century children are used to taking such references not from books at all but from television and film.

One of the Ahlbergs' most successful books is *The Jolly Postman, or Other People's Letters* (1986), where a postman delivers letters, which are physically extracted from 'envelope-pages' in the book and read separately, to fairy-tale and nursery-rhyme characters. The letters demand an extraordinary, street-wise sophistication from the child – the one to Mr Wolf, from Meeny, Miny, Mo & Co Solicitors, on behalf of Miss Riding Hood, threatens him with eviction from her grandmother's cottage; the one to the Witch is a mail order catalogue from Hobgoblin Supplies offering a non-stick cauldron set and gift ideas 'for the wizard in your life'. Children as young as four love this book; seven-year-olds who would now find the literary language and ideas of *Alice* impossibly complex are quite attuned to the cynical, adult nuances of legal and marketing companies. *The Jolly Postman* on the shelf next to *Alice* provides an instant picture of how expectations and images of childhood have become transformed in a century.

Dahl's stories, which are more literary and intended for

older children, often turn on reversed expectations – a giant who is not evil but big and friendly in *The Big Friendly Giant*; a modern witch who is a headmistress in *Matilda*. Some of his characters are descendants of nonsense figures – the carica-tured child couch potato Mike Teevee who is stretched as thin as chewing gum after he has passed through a television screen; the greedy boy Augustus Gloop; the spoilt child Veruca Salt, disposed down a rubbish chute in *Charlie and the Chocolate Factory*. He could invent magical worlds – the chocolate rivers and minty sugar meadows in *Charlie and the Chocolate Factory*, for example – which seemed to emerge not out of nostalgia but out of contemporary children's lives. Dahl's books are original, compelling and anarchic, but he did not create a radical form of literature or a new vision of the world in the way that Carroll or Lear did.

It is no coincidence that children's writers, in Victorian and Edwardian times among the most innovative literary talents, have since the 1930s been marginal literary figures, and that the original voices in English-speaking literature have for much of this century focused on the adolescent or youthful hero. In the mid-twentieth century, childhood, the epitome of innocence and security, was remote from everything English culture idealised and responded to. By the 1950s the romance with childhood was replaced by a love-affair with the adolescent or angry young man, a type much closer to the heart of modern Western culture, who represented what was turbulent and difficult, insecure and cynical, in sophisticated society. The Beatles, pop art, teenyboppers, were just a decade away.

In America, two teenagers, Lolita and Holden Caulfield, were the memorable literary characters of the 1950s, and Nabokov's *Lolita* and Salinger's *Catcher in the Rye* were both great works of literature and radical new departures in the art of fiction. In England their equivalents were Jimmy Porter and Jim Dixon, and again Kingsley Amis's *Lucky Jim* and John Osborne's *Look Back in Anger* were revolutionary in determin-ing the future of the English novel and English drama. Where the Victorian and Edwardians had identified with literature's little girls and boys, Alice and Peter Pan, by the mid-twentieth century Holden Caulfield or Jimmy Porter were the favourite self-portraits of the reading classes. Now the fixation on adolescence has permeated popular fiction, in the same way that images of children permeated sentimental, popular Victorian fiction. The success of books like *The Secret Diary of Adrian Mole aged 13¾* lies in society's adolescent self-image. And yet – there is still a child in all of us, and we return again and again, for comfort and enjoyment, to the children's books that emerged out of the Victorian and Edwardian love-affair with childhood.

Notes

All quotations from Lewis Carroll's diaries are from *The Diaries of Lewis Carroll*, Vols 1 and 2, edited by Roger Lancelyn Green, London, 1953.

All quotations from Lewis Carroll's letters are from *The Collected Letters of Lewis Carroll*, Vols 1 and 2, edited by Morton Cohen with the asisstance of Roger Lancelyn Green, London, 1979.

Introduction

1. Christopher Milne, *The Enchanted Places*, London, 1974, p. 159.

Chapter 1

1. John Ruskin, *Praeterita*, Vol. 3, London, 1899, pp. 54–5.
2. Francis Kilvert, *Diary*, new edition, London, 1992, p. 34; 3 May 1870.
3. Ibid, p. 232; 13 July 1875.
4. Amy Cruse, *Victorians and their Books*, London, 1935, p. 165.
5. G. M. Trevelyan, *English Social History*, London, 1944, p. 545.
6. John Sutherland, *Mrs Humphry Ward, Eminent Victorian, Pre-eminent Edwardian*, Oxford, 1990, p. 59.
7. G. M. Trevelyan, *English Social History*, London, 1944, p. 545.
8. Lewis Carroll to Macmillan, 15 December 1869.
9. Lewis Carroll to Mrs N. H. Stevens, 1 June 1892.
10. Lewis Carroll to Mrs J. Chataway, 28 June 1876.
11. Lewis Carroll to Gertrude Chataway, 21 July 1876.
12. Mrs Gaskell to George Eliot, quoted in Jenny Uglow, *Elizabeth Gaskell: A Habit of Stories*, London, 1993, p. 463.

13. Gay Daly, *Pre-Raphaelites in Love*, London, 1989, p. 310.
14. John Ruskin to Kate Greenaway, July 1883, quoted in Rodney Engen, *Kate Greenaway: A Biography*, London, 1981, p. 95.
15. Michael Mason, *The Making of Victorian Sexuality*, Oxford, 1994, p. 221.

Chapter 2
1. Archdeacon Charles Dodgson to Lewis Carroll, 1840, quoted in Derek Hudson, *Lewis Carroll, An Illustrated Biography*, new edition, London, 1976, p. 35.
2. Recalled by Mary Smedley, aunt of Archdeacon Dodgson, in a letter of 13 February 1851, written after Mrs Dodgson's death, quoted in *The Diaries of Lewis Carroll*, Vol. 1, p. 29.
3. Lewis Carroll, Diaries, Vol. 1, 2 July 1863.
4. Ibid, Vol. 2, 18 February 1886.
5. Ibid, Vol. 1, 21 May 1856.
6. Ibid, 19 December 1857.
7. 'Alice's Recollections of Carrollian Days', *The Cornhill Magazine*, July 1932.
8. Obituary article by the Rev. G. S. Cowley-Brown, quoted in Derek Hudson, *Lewis Carroll: An Illustrated Biography*, p. 63.
9. Lewis Carroll to George Charles Bell, headmaster of Marlborough, 19 February 1882.
10. John Pudney, *Lewis Carroll and his World*, London, 1976, p. 41.
11. Lewis Carroll to Mrs A. L. Moore, 24 July 1896.
12. Lewis Carroll to Mrs A. L. Mayhew, 27 May 1879.
13. Anne Clark, *Lewis Carroll: A Biography*, London, 1979, p. 193.
14. Quoted in *The Collected Letters of Lewis Carroll*, Vol. 1, p. 230.
15. Lewis Carroll to Gertrude Chataway, 13 October 1875.
16. Lewis Carroll to Gertrude Chataway, 28 October 1876.
17. Lewis Carroll to Agnes Hull, 21 April 1881.
18. Lewis Carroll to Emily or Violet Gordon, 14 August 1877.
19. Lewis Carroll to Gertrude Chataway, 2 January 1876.
20. Lewis Carroll to Mrs C. F. Moberley Bell, 27 September 1893.

21. Lewis Carroll to Hilda Moberley Bell, 5 October 1893.
22. Lewis Carroll to Alice (Liddell) Hargreaves, 1 March 1885.
23. Derek Hudson, *Lewis Carroll: An Illustrated Biography*, p. 113.
24. Lewis Carroll, 'Alice on the Stage', in *The Theatre*, April 1887.
25. Lewis Carroll to Mrs A. L. Mayhew, 28 May 1879.
26. Letter from E. K. Jupp, Junior Student at Christchurch, to his brother, 1868, quoted in Derek Hudson, *Lewis Carroll: An Illustrated Biography*, p. 131.
27. Lewis Carroll, 'Alice on the Stage', in *The Theatre*, April 1887.
28. John Pudney, *Lewis Carroll and his World*, p. 76.
29. Lewis Carroll, Diaries, Vol. 1, 25 June 1863.
30. Ibid, 5 December 1863.
31. Ibid, 12 December 1863.
32. Ibid, 12 May 1864.
33. Ibid, 11 May 1865.
34. John Pudney, *Lewis Carroll and his World*, p. 106.
35. Stuart Collingwood, *Life and Letters of Lewis Carroll*, London, 1898, pp. 272–3.
36. Lewis Carroll to F.H. Atkinson, 10 December 1881.
37. Lewis Carroll to Mrs S. Dodgson, 31 July 1890.
38. Lewis Carroll to E. Gertrude Thomson, 2 October 1893.
39. Lewis Carroll to Skeffington Dodgson, 16 February 1893.
40. Lewis Carroll to F. H. Atkinson, 10 December 1898.
41. Lewis Carroll, Diaries, Vol. 2, 1 November 1888.
42. Stuart Collingwood in a letter to Menella Dodgson, 3 February 1932, quoted in Derek Hudson, *Lewis Carroll: An Illustrated Biography*, p. 161.
43. Lewis Carroll, Diaries, Vol. 2, 10 April 1877.
44. Lewis Carroll to E. Gertrude Thomson, 2 October 1893.
45. Lewis Carroll to Mrs N. H. Stevens, 20 October 1892.
46. Ethel Sidgwick quoted in *The Collected Letters of Lewis Carroll*, Vol. 2, p. 906.
47. Lewis Carroll, Diaries, Vol. 2, 18 November 1881.
48. Lewis Carroll to Louisa Dodgson, 28 September 1896.
49. Lewis Carroll to T. Harry Furniss, 29 November 1886.

Chapter 3

1. Mrs Hugh Fraser, *A Diplomat's Wife in Many Lands*, Vol. 2, London, 1910, p. 25.
2. Edward Lear, Diary, 19 June 1871, quoted in Vivien Noakes, *Edward Lear, The Life of a Wanderer*, London, 1968, p. 250.
3. Edward Lear, Diary, 24 March 1877, in Ibid, p. 19.
4. Mrs Wintrop Chanler, *Roman Spring*, Boston, 1934, p. 29.
5. Edward Lear to Ruth Decie, 9 September 1862, in *Edward Lear: Selected Letters*, ed. Vivien Noakes, Oxford, 1988, p. 177.
6. Edward Lear to Miss Coombe, quoted in Angus Davidson, *Edward Lear: Landscape Painter and Nonsense Poet*, London, 1938, p. 17.
7. *Once-a-Week*, 5 January 1867.
8. Edward Lear to Ann Lear, 14 December 1837, in *Edward Lear: Selected Letters,* pp. 33–4.
9. Edward Lear to Emily Tennyson, 10 May 1865, in Ibid, p. 205.
10. Edward Lear to Alfred Tennyson, 9 June 1855, quoted in Vivien Noakes, *Edward Lear: The Life of a Wanderer*, p. 127.
11. Edward Lear to Lady Waldegrave, 24 November 1865, in *Later Letters of Edward Lear*, ed. Lady Strachey, London, 1911, pp. 63–4.
12. Edward Lear to Chichester Fortescue, 21 October 1862, in *Letters of Edward Lear*, ed. Lady Strachey, London, 1907, p. 253.
13. Edward Lear to Evelyn Baring, 1864, in *Edward Lear: Selected Letters,* p. 195.
14. Edward Lear to Ann Lear, 4 April 1849, in Ibid, p. 106.
15. Edward Lear to Emily Tennyson, 9 October 1856, in Ibid, p. 145.
16. Edward Lear to the Earl of Northbrook, 11 October 1867, Ibid, p. 210.
17. Edward Lear to David Morier, 12 January 1871, in Ibid, p. 228.
18. Edward Lear to Chichester Fortescue, 20 April 1862, in *Letters of Edward Lear*, p. 236.
19. Edward Lear to Chichester Fortescue, 31 December 1871, in *Later Letters of Edward Lear*, p. 144.

20. Edward Lear to Chichester Fortescue, 22 August 1868, in Ibid, p. 105.
21. Edward Lear, Diary, 1 August 1874, quoted in Vivien Noakes, *Edward Lear: The Life of a Wanderer*, pp. 268–9.
22. Edward Lear to Chichester Fortescue, 28 October 1878, in *Later Letters of Edward Lear*, p. 213.
23. Edward Lear, Diary, 2 August 1877, quoted in Vivien Noakes, *Edward Lear: The Life of a Wanderer*, p. 277.
24. *Later Letters of Edward Lear*, Preface by Hubert Congreve, pp. 35–6.
25. Edward Lear, Diary, 4 April 1887, quoted in Vivien Noakes, *Edward Lear: The Life of a Wanderer*, p. 309.
26. Letter from Madame Philipp, widow of Dr Hassall, to Lady Strachey, 21 January 1911, in *Later Letters of Edward Lear*, p. 361.

Interlude

1. Iona Opie in an interview with the author, *Financial Times*, 11 May 1991.

Chapter 4

1. George Moore, *Criticisms*, 1895, quoted in Kenneth McConkey, *Edwardian Portraits: Images of an Age of Opulence*, Suffolk, 1987, p. 124.
2. Haldane MacFall, in Ibid, p. 134.
3. Martin Green, *Children of the Sun*, London, new edition, 1992, p. 63.
4. Tim Jeal, *Baden-Powell*, London, 1989, p. 92.
5. Rupert Brooke to Frances Darwin, quoted in Paul Delany, *The Neo-Pagans: Friendship and Love in the Rupert Brooke Circle*, London, 1987, p. 22.
6. J. M. Barrie, *Margaret Ogilvy*, London, 1896, pp. 12–13.
7. Ibid, p. 18.
8. J. M. Barrie to Mrs Fred Oliver, 12 March 1931, quoted in Andrew Birkin, *J. M. Barrie and the Lost Boys*, London, 1979, p. 21.
9. J. M. Barrie, *What Every Woman Knows*, Act 2.
10. Daphne du Maurier, *Gerald, a Portrait*, London, new edition, 1966, p. 110.

11. I am indebted to Martin Green, 'The Charm of Peter Pan', in *Children's Literature*, Vol. 9, 1981, for this comparison.
12. Denis Mackail, *The Story of JMB*, London, 1941, p. 347.
13. Quoted in Andrew Birkin, *J. M. Barrie and the Lost Boys*, p. 297.
14. Dedication to Peter Pan, *The Plays of J. M. Barrie*, London, 1928, p. 5–6.
15. J. M. Barrie to George Llewelyn Davies, 11 March 1915, quoted in Andrew Birkin, *J. M. Barrie and the Lost Boys*, p. 228.
16. Ibid, p. 228.
17. J. M. Barrie, *Courage: The Rectorial Address delivered at St Andrew's University*, 3 May 1922, London, p. 32.
18. Lytton Strachey to Ottoline Morrell, 29 June 1921, quoted in Michael Holroyd, *Lyttoin Strachey*, London, 1971, p. 1025.
19. J. M. Barrie to Elizabeth Lucas, December 1921, quoted in Andrew Birkin, *J. M. Barrie and the Lost Boys*, p. 295.

Chapter 5

1. Henry James to Oliver Wendell Holmes Jnr, quoted in Stanley Weintraub, *Victoria: Biography of a Queen*, London, 1987, p. 641.
2. Peter Green, *Kenneth Grahame: A Biography*, London, 1959, p. 226.
3. Ibid, p. 43.
4. Patrick R. Chalmers, *Kenneth Grahame: Life, Letters and Unpublished Work*, London, 1933, p. 97.
5. Constance Smedley, *Crusaders*, London, 1929, p. 150.
6. Patrick R. Chalmers, *Kenneth Grahame: Life, Letters and Unpublished Work*, p. 97.
7. Kenneth Grahame to Elspeth Thomson, 26 June 1899 and 20 June 1899, quoted in Peter Green, *Kenneth Grahame: A Biography*, p. 227.
8. Kenneth Grahame to Elspeth Thomson, 22 June 1899, in Ibid, p. 213.
9. Kenneth Grahame to Elspeth Thomson, 7 July 1899, in Ibid, p. 216.
10. Ibid, p. 217.
11. Emma Hardy to Elspeth Grahame, 20 August 1899, in Ibid, p. 220.

12. Kenneth Grahame to Mrs Ward, May 1904, in Ibid, p. 232.
13. Kenneth Grahame, edited by Elspeth Grahame, *First Whisper of the Wind in the Willows,* London, 1944, p. 3.
14. Constance Smedley, *Crusaders*, p. 150.
15. Kenneth Grahame, *Bertie's Escapade*, London, 1944, pp. 45–6.
16. Curtis Brown, *Contact*, London, 1934, p. 60.
17. *The Bookman*, January 1909.
18. Peter Green, *Kenneth Grahame: A Biography*, p. 304.
19. E. H. Shepard, 'Illustrating *The Wind in the Willows*', in *The Horn-Book*, April 1954.
20. A. A. Milne, Introduction to 1951 edition of *The Wind in the Willows*.

Chapter 6
1. Christopher Milne, *The Enchanted Places*, London, 1974, p. 103.
2. A. A. Milne to Kenneth Milne, quoted in Ann Thwaite, *A. A. Milne: His Life*, London, 1990, p. 327.
3. A. A. Milne, *By Way of Introduction*, London, 1929, pp. 205–6.
4. Christopher Milne, *The Enchanted Places*, p. 141.
5. Ibid, p. 159.
6. Ann Thwaite, *A. A. Milne: His Life*, p. 362.
7. Christopher Milne, *The Enchanted Places*, p. 146.
8. A. A. Milne, Introduction to 1951 edition of *The Wind in the Willows*.
9. Christopher Milne, *The Enchanted Places*, p. 165.
10. Ibid, pp. 166–7.
11. A. A. Milne to Maud Milne, 9 May 1955, quoted in Ann Thwaite, *A. A. Milne: His Life*, p. 482.
12. *The New Statesman*, 11 September 1939.

Epilogue
1. Paul Webster, *Antoine de Saint-Exupéry: The Life and Death of the Little Prince*, London, 1953, p. 7.

Bibliography

1 Children's books

Ahlberg, Janet and Allan, *Burglar Bill*, London 1977

Ahlberg, Janet and Allan, *The Jolly Postman,* London 1986

Alcott, Louisa, *Little Women*, London 1871

Barrie, J. M., *Peter Pan and Wendy*, London 1911

Barrie, J. M., *The Plays of J. M. Barrie* (including *Peter Pan*), London 1928

Bond, Michael, *A Bear Called Paddington*, London 1958

Burnett, Frances Hodgson, *Little Lord Fauntleroy*, London 1886

Burnett, Francis Hodgson, *The Secret Garden,* London 1911

Carroll, Lewis, *Alice's Adventures in Wonderland,* London 1866

Carroll, Lewis, *The Hunting of the Snark*, London 1876

Carroll, Lewis, *Sylvie and Bruno,* London 1889

Carroll, Lewis, *Sylvie and Bruno Concluded*, London 1893

Carroll Lewis, *Through the Looking-Glass, and What Alice Found There,* London 1872

Dahl, Roald, *The BFG*, London 1982

Dahl, Roald, *Charlie and the Chocolate Factory*, London 1964

Dahl, Roald, *Matilda*, London 1988

Edgeworth, Maria, *The Parent's Assistant*, London 1796

Grahame, Kenneth, *The Wind in the Willows*, London 1908

Hoffman, E. T. A., *Nutcracker*, new edition London 1984

Ingelow, Jean, *Mopsa the Fairy,* London 1869

Kästner, Erich, *Emil and the Detectives*, London 1931

Kingsley, Charles, *The Water Babies*, London 1863

Kipling, Rudyard, *Just So Stories*, London 1902

Kipling, Rudyard, *Puck of Pook's Hill*, London 1906

Kipling, Rudyard, *Stalkey and Co.,* London 1899

Lear, Edward, *A Book of Nonsense*, London 1846

Lear, Edward, *Laughable Lyrics,* London 1877

Lear, Edward, *More Nonsense Pictures, Rhymes, Botany etc.,* London 1872

Lear, Edward, *Nonsense Songs, Stories, Botany and Alphabets,* London 1871

Lewis, C. S., *The Lion, The Witch and the Wardrobe,* London 1950

MacDonald, George, *At the Back of the North Wind,* London 1871

MacDonald, George, *Dealing with the Fairies,* London 1867

Milne, A. A., *The House at Pooh Corner,* London 1928

Milne, A. A., *Now We Are Six,* London 1927

Milne, A. A., *When We Were Very Young,* London 1924

Milne, A. A., *Winnie-the-Pooh,* London 1926

Nesbit, E., *Five Children and It,* London 1902

Nesbit, E., *The Railway Children,* London 1906

Nesbit, E., *The Story of the Treasure Seekers,* London 1899

Norton, Mary, *The Borrowers,* London 1952

ed. Opie, Iona and Peter, *The Oxford Book of Nursery Rhymes,* Oxford 1951

Paget, F. E., *The Hope of the Katzekopfs,* London 1844

Pearce, A. Philippa, *Tom's Midnight Garden,* London 1958

Potter, Beatrix, *The Complete Tales of Beatrix Potter,* new edition London 1989

Rossetti, Christina, *Speaking Likenesses,* London 1874

Ruskin, John, *The King of the Golden River,* London 1851

Saint-Exupéry, Antoine de, *The Little Prince,* London 1934

Sherwood, Mrs, *The Fairchild Family,* London 1818

Sinclair, Catherine, *Holiday House,* Edinburgh 1839

Spyri, Joanna, *Heidi's Early Experiences,* London 1884

Stevenson, R. L., *Treasure Island,* London 1883

Thackeray, William, *The Rose and the Ring,* London 1855

Tolkien, J. R. R., *The Hobbit,* London 1937

Tolkien, J. R. R., *The Lord of the Rings,* second edition London 1966

Wilde, Oscar, *The Happy Prince,* London 1888

2 Letters, diaries, biographies, essays, novels

Barrie, J. M., *Courage: The Rectorial Address delivered at St Andrew's University,* London 1922

Barrie, J. M., *The Little White Bird,* London 1902

Barrie, J. M., *Margaret Ogilvy*, London 1896

Barrie, J. M., *Tommy and Grizel*, London 1900

Birkin, Andrew, *J. M. Barrie and the Lost Boys*, London 1979

Bredsdorff, Elias, *Hans Christian Andersen: A Biography*, Oxford 1975

Brown, Curtis, *Contact*, London 1934

Carroll, Lewis, *The Collected Letters of Lewis Carroll*, ed. Morton N. Cohen, with the assistance of Roger Lancelyn Green, London 1977

Carroll, Lewis, *The Diaries of Lewis Carroll*, ed. Roger Lancelyn Green, London 1953

Chalmers, Patrick, *Kenneth Grahame: Life, Letters and Unpublished Work*, London 1933

Chanler, Mrs Wintrop, *Roman Spring*, Boston 1934

Chitty, Susan, *That Singular Person Called Lear*, London 1988

Clark, Anne, *Lewis Carroll: A Biography*, London 1979

Collingwood, Stuart, *Life and Letters of Lewis Carroll*, London 1898

Daly, Gay, *Pre-Raphaelites in Love,* London 1989

Davidson, Angus, *Edward Lear: Landscape Painter and Nonsense Poet*, London 1938

Delany, Paul, *The Neo-Pagans: Friendship and Love in the Rupert Brooke Circle*, London 1987

du Maurier, Daphne, *Gerald, A Portrait,* London 1934

Engen, Rodney, *Kate Greenaway: A Biography*, London 1981

Fraser, Mrs Hugh, *A Diplomat's Wife in Many Lands*, London 1910

Gattegno, Jean, *Lewis Carroll: A Life*, London 1974

Grahame, Elspeth, *First Whisper of the Wind in the Willows,* London 1944

Grahame, Kenneth, *Bertie's Escapade*, London 1944

Grahame, Kenneth, *Dream Days*, London 1898

Grahame, Kenneth, *The Golden Age*, London 1895

Grahame, Kenneth, *Pagan Papers*, London 1893

Green, Peter, *Kenneth Grahame: A Biography*, London 1959

Holroyd, Michael, *Lytton Strachey*, London 1971

Hudson, Derek, *Lewis Carroll, An Illustrated Biography*, London 1954

Jeal, Tim, *Baden-Powell*, London 1989

Kilvert, Francis, *Diary*, new edition London 1992

Lear, Edward, *Edward Lear, Selected Letters*, ed. Vivien Noakes, Oxford 1988

Lear, Edward, *Later Letters of Edward Lear*, ed. Lady Strachey, London 1911

Lear, Edward, *Letters of Edward Lear*, ed. Lady Strachey, London 1907

Mackail, Denis, *The Story of J.M.B.*, London 1941

Milne, Christopher, *The Enchanted Places*, London 1974

Milne, A. A., *By Way of Introduction*, London 1929

Milne, A. A., *It's Too Late Now*, London 1939

Noakes, Vivien, *Edward Lear: The Life of a Wanderer*, London 1968

Pudney, John, *Lewis Carroll and his World*, London 1976

Ruskin, John, *Praeterita*, London 1899

Smedley, Constance, *Crusaders*, London 1929

Stevenson, Robert Louis, *Virginibus Puerisque*, London 1881

Sutherland, John, *Mrs Humphry Ward, Eminent Victorian, Pre-eminent Edwardian*, Oxford 1990

Thwaite, Ann, *A. A. Milne: His Life*, London 1990

Tomalin, Claire, *The Invisible Woman: The Story of Nelly Ternan and Charles Dickens*, London 1990

Uglow, Jenny, *Elizabeth Gaskell: A Habit of Stories*, London 1993

Webster, Paul, *Antoine de Saint-Exupéry: The Life and Death of the Little Prince*, London 1993

Weintraub, Stanley, *Victoria, Biography of a Queen*, London 1987

3 Critical works on children's literature

Aries, Philippe, *Centuries of Childhood*, New York 1962

ed. Avery, Gillian, and Briggs, Julia, *Children and their Books*, Oxford 1989

Bettelheim, Bruno, *The Uses of Enchantment*, London 1976

Carpenter, Humphrey, *Secret Gardens*, London 1985

Carpenter, Humphrey, and Pritchard, Mari, *The Oxford Companion to Children's Literature*, Oxford 1984

Cohen, Morton N., *Lewis Carroll: Interviews and Recollections*, London 1989

Coveney, Peter, *The Image of Childhood*, revised edition London 1967

Egan, Michael, 'The Neverland of Id: Barrie, Peter Pan and Freud', in *Children's Literature, the Annual of the Modern*

*Language Association Seminar on Children's Literature, Volume
10*, Philadelphia 1982

Egoff, Sheila, *Worlds Within: Children's Fantasy from the Middle
Ages to Today*, London 1988

Empson, William, 'The Child as Swain' in *Some Versions of
Pastoral*, London 1935

ed. Gardner, Martin, *The Annotated Alice*, New York 1960

Green, Martin, 'The Charm of Peter Pan' in *Children's
Literature, the Annual of the Modern Language Association
Seminar on Children's Literature, Volume 9*, Philadelphia
1981

Helson, Ravenna, 'The Psychological Origins of Fantasy for
Children in Mid-Victorian England', in *Children's Literature,
the Annual of the Modern Language Association Seminar on
Children's Literature, Volume 3*, Philadelphia 1974

ed. Holdsworth, Sara, and Crossley, Joan, *Innocence and
Experience: Images of Children in British Art from 1600 to the
Present*, Manchester 1992

Huxley, Francis, *The Raven and the Writing Desk*, London 1976

Kuznets, Lois R., 'Toad Hall Revisited', in *Children's Literature,
the Annual of the Modern Language Association Seminar on
Children's Literature, Volume 7*, Philadelphia 1978

Lurie, Alison, *Don't Tell the Grown-Ups*, London 1990

Neubauer, John, *The Fin-de-Siècle Culture of Adolescence*,
London 1992

ed. Phillips, Robert, *Aspects of Alice*, London 1972

Rose, Jacqueline, *The Case of Peter Pan*, London 1984

Sale, Roger, *Fairy Tales and After*, Harvard 1978

ed. Sothebys, *Childhood* (Catalogue for a loan exhibition of
Paintings and Works of Art, London 1988)

Steedman, Carolyn, *The Tidy House*, London 1982

Zipes, Jack, *Victorian Fairy Tales: The Revolt of the Fairies and
Elves*, New York 1987

4 Other works

Crews, Frederick C., *The Pooh Perplex*, London 1964

Cruse, Amy, *Victorians and their Books*, London 1935

Green, Martin, *Children of the Sun*, London 1977

Marcus, S., *The Other Victorians: A Study of Sexuality and*

Pornography in mid-Nineteenth Century England, London 1966

Mason, Michael, *The Making of Victorian Sexuality*, Oxford 1994

McConkey, Kenneth, *Edwardian Portraits: Images of an Age of Opulence,* Suffolk 1987

Trevelyan, G. M., *English Social History*, London 1944

Index

Index

Index